BORN TO
BE WILD

DK LONDON
Senior Editor Shaila Brown
US Editor Megan Douglass
Senior Art Editor Smiljka Surla
Designer Anna Pond
Picture Researcher Laura Barwick
Illustrator Sanya Jain

Managing Editor Rachel Fox
Managing Art Editor Owen Peyton Jones
Production Editor Robert Dunn
Senior Production Controller Meskerem Berhane
DTP Designer Jagtar Singh
Jacket Designer Stephanie Tan
Jackets Design Development Manager Sophia MTT

Publisher Andrew Macintyre
Art Director Karen Self
Associate Publishing Director Liz Wheeler
Publishing Director Jonathan Metcalf

Written by John Woodward and Caroline Stamps
Consultant Derek Harvey

First American Edition, 2022
Published in the United States by DK Publishing
1450 Broadway, Suite 801, New York, NY 10018

A catalog record for this book
is available from the Library of Congress.
ISBN 978-0-7440-5137-7

DK books are available at special discounts when
purchased in bulk for sales promotions, premiums,
fund-raising, or educational use. For details, contact:
DK Publishing Special Markets, 1450 Broadway,
Suite 801, New York, NY 10018
SpecialSales@dk.com

Printed and bound in China

For the curious
www.dk.com

MIX
Paper from
responsible sources
FSC™ C018179

This book was made with Forest Stewardship Council ™ certified paper—
one small step in DK's commitment to a sustainable future.

For more information go to www.dk.com/our-green-pledge

BORN TO BE WILD

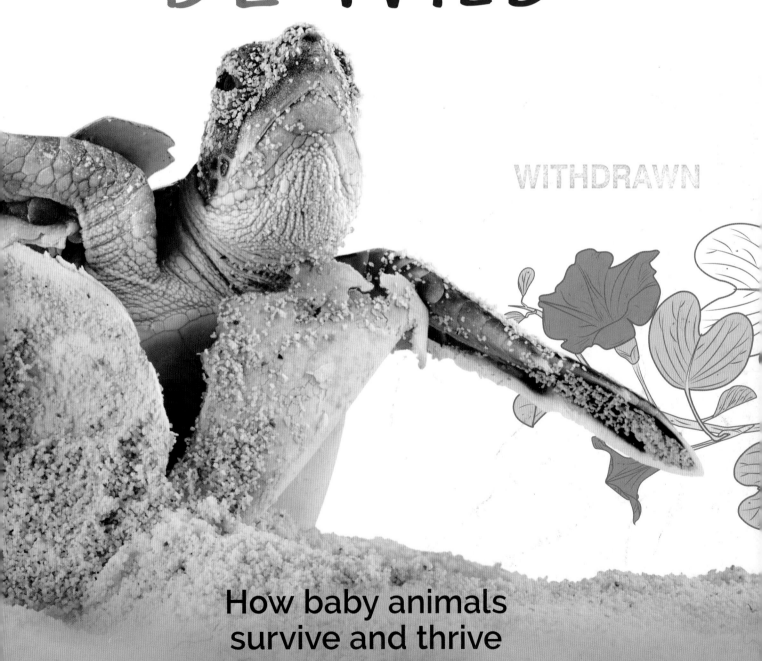

How baby animals survive and thrive

CONTENTS

BRINGING UP BABY

A female orangutan usually has just one baby at a time, and does not have another for at least six years. This allows her to devote all her attention to protecting and teaching each infant, giving it an excellent start in life. Such parental care is typical of highly intelligent animals, including apes and elephants, which are able to learn new skills, such as where to find food, and commit them to memory.

Provided its forest habitat stays intact, this baby orangutan has a good chance of living for 30 years or more.

Eggs and babies

Most female animals lay eggs that contain the developing babies, like these frog's eggs. Those of birds and reptiles have tough, waterproof shells to stop them drying out. But some, like most mammals, retain their young in their bodies until they have developed into fully formed babies.

Helpless or active?

Many small birds, and some other animals such as bears, produce young that are naked, blind, and almost helpless at first, so they need a lot of parental care. Other animals, such as antelope and ducks, are born or hatch in a well-developed active state that enables them to take care of themselves.

STARTING OUT

For many baby animals, life is a lottery. Their mothers produce huge numbers of eggs or young, and abandon them to their fate. Most get eaten by other animals, and very few survive. But some types of animal have a different strategy. They produce just a few babies at a time, and take care of them. As they grow, some of these young animals are taught vital lessons by the adults, which vary depending on where they live.

Metamorphosis
However helpless, a baby bird or mammal is recognizable as a miniature version of its parents. But many other animals, including butterflies, hatch in a quite different form called a larva. The butterfly larva, or caterpillar, has to go through a dramatic change known as metamorphosis to become an adult.

Instinct and learning
All animals start life with a set of instincts that help them survive. Baby spiders are even able to spin webs to catch prey. But animals with big brains, like this cheetah cub, rely more on learning as they grow up. Through copying its mother, and making mistakes, it keeps developing and improving its skills.

MAMMALS

Like all mammals, this mother meerkat feeds her pups on her milk until they are old enough to eat solid food. This means that every young mammal lives with its mother—if not a whole family—for weeks, months, or even years. Protected from danger by the adults, it has plenty of time to learn the lessons and skills that will help keep it safe and well for the rest of its life.

Cubs have a thicker coating of fur, called a mantle, that covers the back of their neck and upper back like a cape. This fur disappears by the time they are two years old.

Black tear marks run from the corners of the cub's eyes—the markings may help protect the eyes from the sun's glare.

The last section of the tail has black rings that get more prominent as the cheetah cub ages.

Unlike other cats, the claws are less retractable—they cannot be pulled in, providing a firm grip on the ground when the cub is running.

A cheetah's coat has around 2,000 black spots, but these can be indistinct on a cub's coat.

Teething time
A cub's teeth begin to appear by around three weeks of age and, as with human babies, when the teeth begin to break through the gums it can cause a little pain. A cub clamps down on a piece of wood to ease that pain.

CHEETAH

Cheetah cubs grow to be the fastest of all land animals

Cheetah cubs are born helpless. Their eyes don't open for the first few days of their lives and they weigh about 10 oz (300 g)—less than a can of tomatoes! The tiny cubs are hidden away among the tall grass of the African savanna, and closely guarded by their mother, who will move them regularly to a new hideout so they are not detected by predators, including lions and hyenas. But despite all her efforts, very few cubs survive into adulthood.

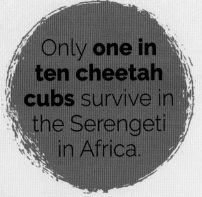

Only **one in ten cheetah cubs** survive in the Serengeti in Africa.

Hunting practice
Cheetah cubs need to be taught how to hunt prey so they can fend for themselves. They accompany their mother on hunting trips when they are a few months old, but the mother also catches live prey for her cubs to practice on. The cubs chase and pounce on their prey to improve their hunting skills.

FAST AND SLEEK

Cheetahs are built for speed—they have long strides, which lengthen as they grow older, and a very flexible spine that allows them to stretch their legs out so they can run faster. They also have sleek bodies and powerful leg muscles. Even as cubs, they can outrun their prey and as adults they can reach speeds of 60 mph (100 kph), making them the fastest land animal in the world.

PLAYTIME WITH MOM

A cheetah mother has between one and eight cubs in a litter. She is responsible for taking care of them, keeping them safe, and teaching them how to hunt and how to stay away from danger. The cubs also play a lot, chasing, catching, and pouncing on each other and on mom!

COAT PATTERN

Newborn
In the first couple of days after birth, a pup's fur has a yellow-white tinge, due to staining by fluid before its birth. After that the fur turns white and the pup is known as a "whitecoat."

Juvenile
After two to three weeks, the white fur begins to fall away, or molt. Harp seals continue to molt once a year throughout their lives. Juveniles have a silver-gray coat with dark spots.

Adult
When fully grown, the harp seal shows why it is so named. The males have a harp-shaped marking across their backs (females don't always have this).

HARP SEAL

Harp seals are born on ice and are left to fend for themselves shortly after birth

For the harp seal, producing a baby at the top of the world means giving birth on floating ice that stretches over the Arctic Ocean in the bitterly cold polar winter. Here, when the extent of the ice reaches its peak, mothers-to-be haul themselves out of the water in their thousands. Incredibly, the pups are fed with milk for just 12 days—one of the shortest nursing periods of any mammal.

A young harp seal pup needs a thick coat because it is born without a layer of fatty blubber under its skin, which will only develop as it grows older.

WARM COAT

Harp seal pups are born with a thick white coat of fine hairs that is especially good at keeping body heat trapped inside. This insulation is lost if their coat gets wet, so they wait a few weeks for their shorter adult coat to develop before plunging into the Arctic Ocean.

Rich milk

The harp seal's milk is so rich that a pup can gain about 5 lb (2. kg) of weight every day. The mother does not lose a lot of weight while nursing as she continues to hunt for fish—unlike other seal mothers, which don't eat at all during this time.

A harp seal's eyes lack tear ducts that drain away tears, so a seal often looks as if it has been crying.

DIVING FOR FISH

When the mother harp seal leaves her newborn on the ice, the vulnerable baby survives on its body fat while it waits the few weeks needed to grow a thinner adult coat suitable for diving. Only then, having lost 50 percent of its body weight, can the hungry pup plunge into the sea for fish—its first solid meal.

ELEPHANT

A baby elephant stays with its mother for many years as it learns vital life skills

The biggest of all living land animals, elephants are also some of the most intelligent, with good memories and excellent problem-solving abilities. Elephants live as long as people, with equally long childhoods. This gives them plenty of time to learn the skills they need to survive in the tropical forests and grasslands of Africa and southern Asia.

FIRST STEPS

An elephant calf can walk within an hour of birth and is highly mobile within 24–48 hours. However, the calf still needs the reassuring guidance of its mother's trunk as it makes its way through its grassland habitat.

The big ears of an African elephant act like radiators, losing excess body heat.

Tusks

An elephant's tusks are elongated front teeth. They appear soon after it is born, and keep growing throughout its life. A baby elephant watches its mother to see how she uses them for stripping edible bark or digging up plant roots. Both the male and female African elephants have tusks.

Trunk

A baby elephant also learns from its mother how to master the art of using its trunk. Strong, flexible, and very sensitive, it can gather food from the ground or trees, suck up water, make trumpeting calls, and even act as a breathing tube when crossing a deep river.

Sturdy legs will one day have to support the weight of the world's heaviest land animal.

The short tusks of this female show that she is still quite young.

A gentle nudge from its mother's trunk helps the baby on its way.

An elephant calf has a sparse coat of brown or rusty-red hair, which diminishes into adulthood.

WRINKLES AND CRACKS

As a baby elephant gets older, its skin gets thicker and wrinkled, with a network of deep cracks. This is because lots of dead skin builds up on the surface over time instead of flaking away.

Hair

Newborn skin
The skin of a baby elephant is bumpy but not very thick. The bumps, each called a papilla, are formed in a layer of living skin and covered by a layer of partly dead skin, which protects the living layer from scratches and grazes.

Thick dead skin layer

Adult skin
As the elephant gets older, the layer of dead skin gets thicker, more wrinkled, and cracked. The cracks fill with water and mud when the elephant bathes, which helps stop sunburn and keeps the elephant cool.

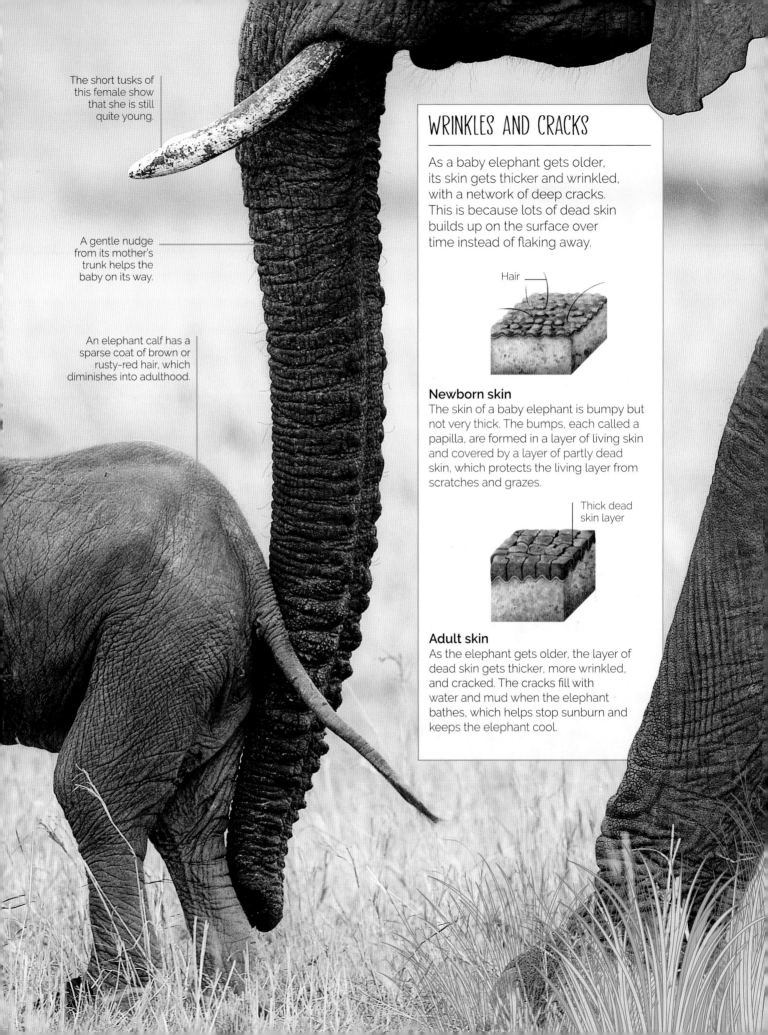

HERD LIFE

African elephants grow up in herds made up of related females and their calves. Each herd is led by the matriarch, the most experienced female in the group, who knows where to find food and water—but all the adults help teach and protect the calves. Young females stay with the herd, but males leave when they are old enough.

WARM AND SAFE

Sea otters have the thickest fur of any animal, with up to one million hairs growing from each square inch of skin. The dense fur keeps the otter warm in the cold seawater, but only if it is properly groomed. Cubs rely on their mothers to do this for them.

Staying afloat

A mother sea otter spends hours every day grooming her cub's fur to make it clean, dry, and fluffy. This makes it trap a layer of air, which keeps the cub warm by stopping the cold water reaching its skin. But the air also acts like a life jacket, making the cub so buoyant that it bobs around on the surface. It can even fall asleep with no risk of drowning while its mother spends time away.

Security blanket

The shallow coastal waters of the North Pacific contain thick underwater forests of giant kelp, a type of seaweed that grows up from the seabed. Sea otters wrap the long kelp fronds around themselves and their cubs to make sure they are not swept away by currents as they sleep on the water. The otters also hunt underwater among the kelp, searching for spiny sea urchins, fish, and other animals.

PROTECTIVE MOM

A mother sea otter usually has a single pup each year, allowing her to give it all her attention. The pup certainly needs it, because at first it cannot swim and spends most of its time clinging to its mother's belly fur. She keeps a tight grip as it sleeps, feeding it on her rich milk when it wakes. She must keep this up for several months, only leaving the pup to float by itself for short periods as she searches for prey.

At birth, a sea otter has a thick coat of fluffy fur. This keeps it warm and, just as importantly, keeps it afloat.

A sea otter may spend up to **four hours** a day grooming its cub's fur.

SEA OTTER

Mother sea otters are devoted to their furry cubs.

Unlike other otters, the sea otter of the coastal North Pacific Ocean spends its entire life at sea—hunting, eating, sleeping, and even giving birth in the water. Their cubs are born with thick fur coats, and these trap so much air that the babies float like corks. This keeps them safe while their mothers hunt for food near the seabed.

A sea otter pup spends a lot of time asleep on its mother's belly.

Long, sensitive whiskers allow the otter to feel for prey in deep, dark water.

GORILLA

A young gorilla stays with its mother until her next baby is born

The biggest and most powerful primate is a sociable species that lives in the forests of Central Africa. Baby gorillas benefit from devoted parents. They live in family groups led by a dominant male, who mates with multiple females and so fathers all the offspring of the group. He protects the group from danger, while mothers concentrate on raising the babies.

STAYING WITH MOM

The mother and baby gorilla form a close bond. The newborn gorilla grips tightly to its mother's chest until it grows big enough to nestle down on her back. This allows them to travel together in safety and comfort. Only the arrival of another baby after several years will limit the time spent together, but the pair still maintain a strong bond.

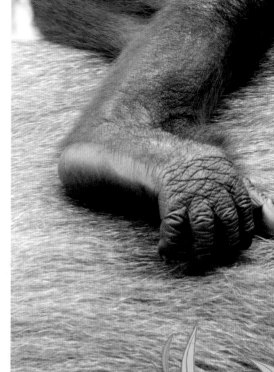

The safest place for the tiny baby gorilla is on its mother's back.

NEW LIFE

A female gorilla can start to breed when she is between eight and ten years old. On average, she becomes pregnant once every four years. The fetus grows slowly inside the mother's womb until the baby is born after eight and a half months. The newborn gorilla is about half the weight of a human baby. Soon its sparse fur will grow thicker.

Like other mammals, the baby develops inside the mother's womb.

The baby receives its nourishment from the placenta.

Who's who?

Gorilla groups contain an average of 10 adults, but sometimes there are more than 20 individuals. Each troop is led by a dominant silverback, an older male gorilla named after the strip of silvery fur that grows in later life. The rest of the group is made up of younger males, known as blackbacks, adult females, and their babies.

Mother gorillas have only **three or four babies** during their lifetime.

PRIMATE PLAYMATES

Just like you, young gorillas enjoy playing together within their troop. They take part in a variety of games, including pretend fighting, wrestling bouts, and playing chase. In quieter moments, they are openly affectionate by giving hugs, sharing snacks, or grooming each other.

Head first
A giraffe calf enters the world with its face and front legs stretched forward. With a long neck and sharp hooves, this helps both the mother and baby avoid injury.

The drop
The calf falls to the ground from a height of about 6 ft (2 m). The tumble doesn't hurt the baby, which lands on its head. Instead, the thump from the fall helps the calf take its first breath.

The first steps
With predators all around, there's no time to rest. Within an hour of being born, the calf must learn to stand, walk, and even run.

GIRAFFE
The tallest babies on Earth

It's tough to find a more impressive baby than a giraffe calf. From the moment it is born, the newborn is about 6 ft (1.8 m) tall—the same height as the average adult man. And even though it is born with legs like stilts, the calf learns how to walk and run within an hour of birth—it needs to learn fast to keep up with its mother for protection against predators.

NECK BONES

A long neck allows a giraffe to eat foods high up in the canopy that other animals can't reach. But when it comes to giving birth, it can pose a problem for the giraffe mother—she has to give birth standing up so the baby's long neck doesn't get damaged in the process.

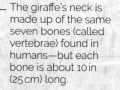

The giraffe's neck is made up of the same seven bones (called vertebrae) found in humans—but each bone is about 10 in (25 cm) long.

Protective mother

Despite their size, giraffe calves are easy targets for lions, crocodiles, and leopards, so mother giraffes always keep a watchful eye for danger. Their height enables them to spot predators in the distance. They also usually sleep while standing up and only nod off for a few minutes at a time. If a predator gets too close, the mother lashes out with powerful kicks from her hind legs.

Baby giraffes have soft, hornlike growths on their heads called ossicones. They harden as they get older—rival male giraffes use them like clubs when fighting.

Tongue-tied

A giraffe's highly flexible, blue-black tongue helps it grab and strip leaves from trees. By the time it is an adult, the calf's tongue is about 20 in (50 cm) long.

Baby giraffes have shorter necks in proportion to their body than adults.

GENTLE GIANTS

A mother giraffe carries her young for about 15 months. She gives birth, usually to one calf, away from the herd. She licks the baby clean before encouraging it to stand by gently nuzzling the newborn. Later, mother and baby rejoin the herd, and the group of giraffe mothers often take turns watching each other's calves.

A baby giraffe's height **doubles** in its first year.

NURSERY HERD

After the first few days of a baby giraffe's life, the mother and calf join other females and their young to form a nursery herd. As they feed together, the mothers stay alert for lions and other predators. The more adults keeping watch, the better the calves' chances of surviving.

POLAR BEAR

Cubs emerge from their snow den in spring

Specially adapted to survive the bitterly cold climate of the far north, polar bears live all around the Arctic Ocean where they hunt seals and other animals on the thick sea ice. The females return to land to have their young, but as soon as the cubs are able to leave their nursery den their mother leads them out onto the ice to teach them how to hunt for themselves.

Warm coat
A single hair, sliced through, reveals a hollow core that traps extra air for better insulation—helping the bear survive temperatures falling to −58°F (−50°C) in winter.

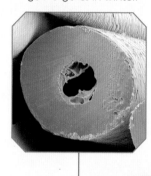

A short, thick, inner layer of fur traps air, even when swimming, helping to keep the cubs warm.

SNOW DEN

In the fall, a pregnant female polar bear builds a den in a snowdrift where she will spend the winter half asleep, living off food reserves built up during the summer. Here, in midwinter, she gives birth to her cubs. Snowfall seals the entrance, keeping out the freezing wind, so the den is much warmer than the world outside.

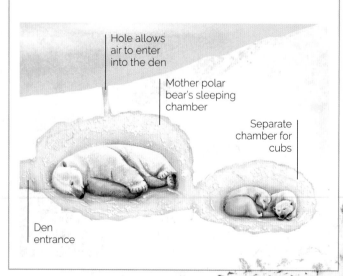

Hole allows air to enter into the den

Mother polar bear's sleeping chamber

Separate chamber for cubs

Den entrance

Icy home

Polar bears hunt mainly on the drifting pack ice of shallow coastal seas. They favor places where the ice is dotted with stretches of open water that attract their main prey, seals. But they also venture onto Arctic islands, where the mother bear sometimes carries her cubs on her back when crossing deep snow.

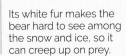

Its white fur makes the bear hard to see among the snow and ice, so it can creep up on prey.

GROWING UP

At birth the cubs are blind, toothless, and incredibly small—each cub is no bigger than one of its mother's paws. But as they feed on her rich milk they grow rapidly until they are big enough to leave the den in spring.

Life lessons

As the polar bear family moves out onto the sea ice in spring, the mother starts hunting again, targeting seals and their pups. Her cubs still rely on her milk, but they watch as she hunts and, over time, learn how it's done. Meanwhile, they gradually eat more meat, both from fresh kills and from carcasses like this dead whale.

Sea bears

Polar bears are good swimmers. Adults can swim for hours, covering 30 miles (50 km) or more. The cubs learn how to swim from their mothers, but can only make short journeys because they do not have as much fat beneath their skin to keep them warm in the water. If they are forced to swim long distances, some may not survive.

ARCTIC LIFE

The tiny cubs—usually twins—are born in winter in a snow den sheltered from the bitter Arctic wind. They live on the mother polar bear's milk until spring, when they follow her out onto the frozen ocean. The cubs stay with her for the first two and a half years of their lives, roaming over the pack ice while they learn how to catch their prey.

SNOW CUBS

Safe in the snow den made by their mother, these three-month-old polar bear cubs are almost old enough to start exploring their icy Arctic home. For the first two weeks they don't go far, playing in the snow while their mother keeps watch, and slipping back into the den to sleep.

GIANT PANDA

A baby giant panda has to get used to spending most of its life eating

Found in the mountain forests of central China, the giant panda is a type of bear that specializes in eating bamboo, a form of grass. This is a poor diet for a bear, so it has to eat a huge quantity of bamboo every day. Even so, a mother panda can only eat enough to produce milk for one cub at a time. If she has twins, the strongest cub leaves very little milk for the other one, which is unlikely to survive.

BAMBOO DIET

A giant panda has big, flattened molars and huge jaw muscles for chewing bamboo to a pulp, and a special thumb-like adaptation in each front paw for gripping the stems. But its digestive system is like that of any other bear, and not well equipped for processing leafy food. It can extract only a few nutrients from each mouthful, so the panda has to spend at least 12 hours a day eating.

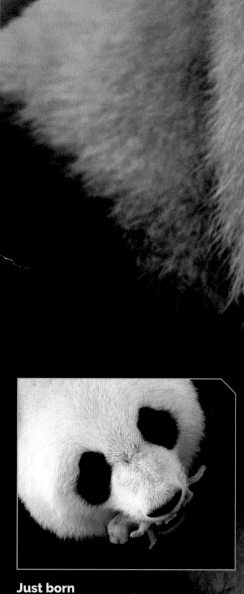

Just born
A panda cub is born blind, toothless, and with almost-naked pink skin. Even at this stage its mother may decide to move to another den, carrying the baby in her mouth. By three weeks old the cub has black and white fur like its mother. It relies on her milk for six months before it starts eating bamboo.

PROTECTIVE MOM

A baby panda stays with its mother for at least 18 months. She feeds it on her milk while it gets used to eating bamboo, which can take a year. She also protects it from wild dogs, snow leopards, eagles, and other hungry predators. They might try to sneak up on a cub, but would not dare attack an adult giant panda.

A baby panda weighs **900** times less than its mother at birth.

The black and white coat makes the panda hard to spot in a shady forest.

Thick fur helps the panda keep warm in its snowy mountain habitat.

TIME FOR PLAY

While its mother is gathering bamboo, a giant panda cub may have time to play in the trees. This helps it learn to balance and climb, using its sharp claws to grip the bark. Escaping into a tree could save its life if it is threatened by a predator, but adults spend most of their time on the ground.

MEERKAT

Meerkats live in big family groups

Meerkats live in the deserts and grasslands of southern Africa, where they form tight-knit family groups of up to 40 individuals called mobs, clans, or gangs. A dominant pair produces most of the babies, and other adults take turns to babysit or stand as a lookout to warn of approaching danger. Some of the older meerkats also teach the young how to hunt.

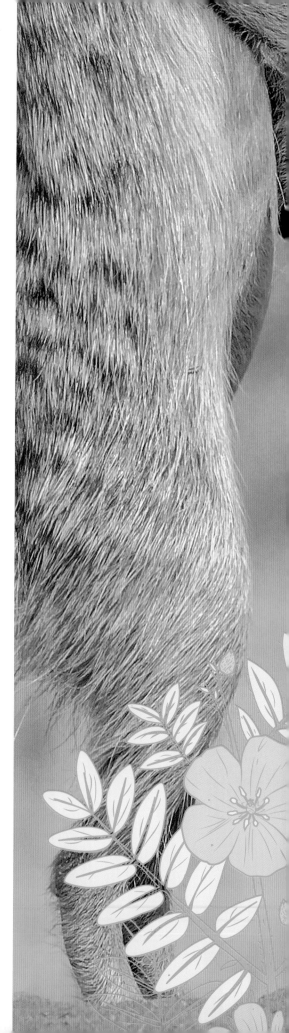

UNDERGROUND HOME

Meerkats are excellent diggers but they often take over burrows dug by other animals. Meerkat babies, called pups, are born in the nursery chamber, which is positioned deep underground where the temperature is constant—not too hot during the day or too cold at night. Here the newborn pups are cared for by everyone, including the dad and older siblings.

A meerkat pup emerges from the burrow when it is about 3–4 weeks old.

A lookout watches for predators.

A pup cries if it is hungry.

A meerkat pup is so **tiny**, it can fit in the palm of your hand.

Scorpion school

To teach the pups how to safely eat a scorpion, an older meerkat will catch and kill a scorpion for the little ones to eat. Next, the pups are given a live scorpion with its venomous stinger bitten off. Through practice, the pups soon learn to catch and kill scorpions on their own.

A meerkat can close its small ears tightly to keep out sand and dirt.

Thin fur on its head and back allows a meerkat to keep cool.

BABYSITTERS

Every morning, the meerkat family emerges from its burrow to warm up in the sun. While some meerkats go out in search of food, others stay with the youngest members of the mob, looking out for danger. If a predator approaches, the lookout gives a warning cry and all the meerkats dive for cover.

Forward-facing eyes help a meerkat judge distances and scan the horizon for predators.

WALKABOUT

A few weeks after being born, a meerkat pup is ready to venture out of the burrow during the day, keeping constant watch for predators such as snakes, jackals, and birds of prey. If the pup has no time to dive under cover, an adult member rushes over to shield it from the enemy.

PANGOLIN

Young pangolins munch through thousands of ants and termites every day for survival

Pangolins are protected by extraordinary armor from head to tail. Strong scales shield the entire body against attack in the forests and grasslands of Asia and Africa. However, it is a different story for baby pangolins. Their soft pink scales leave them vulnerable. Newborns rely on their mothers to take care of them until their scales toughen up over time.

HITCHING A RIDE

Pangolin pregnancies vary from three to five months, depending upon species. Females give birth to a single baby called a pangopup. It is as light as a can of soup and the length of a pencil. The mother feeds her newborn milk for at least three months. When she forages for food at night, the pangopup stays close by, riding on her back until it can walk independently.

Pangolins are the **only mammals** covered in scales.

Safe sleeping
Pangolins sleep in underground burrows or curl up on the forest floor, using the fallen leaves as camouflage. When the pangopup is very young, the mother wraps her body tightly around her baby to make a protective barrier. Older pangopups sleep alongside the mother, with them both curling up separately into solid balls to deter predators.

Tongue twisting
Although pangolins have no teeth, they have long, sticky, flexible tongues attached to their rib cages that extend to lick ants and termites from deep inside their nests. Pangopups learn how to do this from their mothers when they are only about one month old.

Scales are made of keratin, the same material in human hair and fingernails.

Sharp claws are used to cling onto its mother's back and to tear open ant and termite nests.

LEMUR

Lemur babies cry out with simple squeaks before learning a more extensive language

Ring-tailed lemurs live in Madagascar, an island off the east coast of Africa. The young, or pups, are born into large, noisy groups that are constantly communicating. The pups soon join in, calling to their mothers. Before long, they will learn more than 28 different sounds— each with a specific meaning.

The baby is born with blue eyes, but they turn yellow as it grows older.

HOLDING ON

A lemur mother usually gives birth to one infant that weighs less than 3½ oz (100 g). For the first couple of weeks, the newborn clings to its mother's tummy. After that, it moves onto her back, gripping tightly with its hands and feet.

Lemurs **eat soil** for extra minerals.

Lemurs have dense gray-brown fur.

EXPLORING THE WORLD

Baby lemurs, like lots of mammal young, are playful and inquisitive. They stay close to their mothers, but gradually venture further afield. Adult female lemurs often share childcare, so the youngsters have plenty of supervision. Sometimes, females without infants of their own are so persistent in wanting to babysit that they may kidnap babies and not give them back.

Cleaning time

Ring-tailed lemurs have two tongues— a smaller, lighter pink tongue underneath the main tongue is used for grooming, along with their comblike lower front teeth. Mom cuddles and grooms her baby regularly, and it is also groomed by other females.

Climbing

Although comfortable on the ground, where they look for fruit and insects to feed on, ring-tailed lemurs spend more than half of their life in the trees. So young lemurs have to learn to climb, and it's a skill they learn quickly. By four weeks, a pup is clambering and leaping around fearlessly, using its long tail for balance. At night, they stay in the treetops, where they sleep with the rest of the family.

TROOP LIFE

Ring-tailed lemurs spend more time on the ground than other lemur species. They live in troops of up to 30 individuals. As pups, they learn by riding on their mother's back and watching what she does. The females remain in the troop into which they are born for life, but the males move into a new troop after they reach maturity.

BAT-EARED FOX

The male bat-eared fox plays a key role in bringing up his family

The tropical grasslands of Africa swarm with insects, especially termites. They are so abundant that the bat-eared fox eats nothing else. It is specialized for the job with huge ears for detecting its prey in the grass and even underground. The adult foxes teach their young how to do this by taking them on family hunting trips.

YOUNG FAMILY

Bat-eared foxes live in family burrows that they dig themselves. The burrows act as nursery dens, where the female has her cubs and feeds them on her milk. But she must eat a lot to keep up her milk supply, so she is often away hunting. This means she relies on the male's parental care. He grooms the cubs, keeps them warm at night, and defends the den from predators.

These day-old pups will rely on their mother's milk for up to 15 weeks.

Playful pups
Like many baby animals, the young pups play together, chasing around the burrow entrance and ambushing each other in rough and tumble games. This helps the pups learn the skills they will need to survive on the open plains when they grow up.

The fox's enormous ears act as radiators, losing excess heat on hot days.

BUSY DAY

As the pups get older, the family often hunt together because a big termite colony provides plenty of food for all. This enables the adult foxes to teach the young what to eat, and how to catch it.

Insect prey

The big ears of a bat-eared fox can detect the slightest rustle of an insect moving through the dry soil beneath its feet. Its pup can hear it, too, and watches carefully as the adult digs out its prey and eats it, chewing very rapidly with its many small teeth to reduce it to a pulp. Before long, the pup will be able to find its own prey without the help of its parents.

Moving house

Each family of bat-eared foxes digs several dens within its grassland territory. If one den is threatened by predators or in danger of collapse, an adult—usually the male—will move the pups to a different burrow network. He has to move them one by one, picking up each pup in his jaws and carrying it to the new den before returning for another.

TEAMWORK

Stalking
The lionesses do all the hunting, working together. Cubs learn to hunt by watching them—initially by learning to stalk.

Chasing
The victim is usually young, or old and weak. The lioness grabs with its claws, trying to unbalance its prey.

Ambush
Other lionesses look for opportunities to jump in and ambush the prey. It's a tricky skill for the cubs to pick up.

Sharing
Prides share their kills, but there's an eating order. A male usually eats first while cubs will be left until last.

LION

Lion cubs learn their survival skills through play

These huge cats are the only ones to live in groups called prides. A pride may have around six lions, consisting of related females, their young, and one or a few males who defend their pride. After the first few weeks of life, cubs are often raised in crèches and cared for by the entire pride.

Lion cubs have spotted coats but the spots begin to fade within weeks. Faint spots can still be seen on the legs of juveniles.

Lions have black markings on the backs of their ears. It is thought this may help with hunting, as a "follow me" signal.

Each front paw has an extra digit, a dewclaw. These help a lion grip prey.

Protective mom

A lioness looks for a secluded place away from the pride to give birth to up to six cubs. They are hidden in dense undergrowth for the first few weeks of their lives, the mother only leaving them to hunt. If they stray, she will carry them back to safety. The cubs are cared for by their mother until they are ready to join the pride at around six weeks old.

PLAY FIGHTING

Like many young mammals, lion cubs love to play. They stalk, pounce, and grasp each other, rolling around and nipping tails and ears. It's an important way for them to bond, but also helps develop their strength and coordination in readiness for hunting.

TIME FOR REST

Lions happily spend up to 20 hours
a day resting. Cubs have other ideas;
they often want to play. Their coats
blend into the grassy plains, helping
protect them if the adults are asleep.
Cubs are vulnerable to attack from
hyenas, birds of prey, and even male
lions from other prides.

Safe refuge
Most adult brown bears are too heavy to climb trees. But bear cubs do not have this problem and can easily scramble up a tree, which can be a safe refuge from enemies, such as wolves.

FAMILY OUTING

Brown bears have a broad diet of berries, nuts, juicy roots, insects, fish, and meat, so the bear cubs have a lot to learn about what to eat and where to find it. Their mother teaches them by example, living with them as a family for about two and a half years.

BROWN BEAR

Bear cubs are taught life skills by their mother

Living in the northern forests and mountains of North America, Europe, and Asia, the brown bear is one of the biggest and most powerful bears. Known as the grizzly bear in parts of North America, it has a ferocious reputation. But the females are devoted mothers, protecting their cubs and teaching them all they need to know to survive.

A brown bear cub locates most of its food by scent and sound, since its vision is not very good.

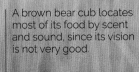

EARLY DAYS

A female brown bear usually has two or three cubs at a time. Born early in the year in her winter den, the tiny newborns are naked, blind, toothless, and helpless. She must keep them warm, safe, and well fed on her milk, which is enriched by her stored fat reserves. This fat-rich milk is more than five times richer than cow's milk, making the bear cubs gain weight very quickly.

Mother's milk
The cubs feed only on their mother's milk until the beginning of summer, when the family emerges from the den and the cubs start trying solid foods. Feeding the cubs over a long period of time impacts the mother, because she does not eat while she is hidden away over the winter. She may lose almost half her body weight. However, she cannot leave the cubs alone in the den while she finds food because they are so underdeveloped.

Fearless fighter
The mother bear is fearless in defense of her cubs. Their most deadly enemies are other bears, especially adult males who may kill the cubs. But the mother will fight a male up to twice her own weight, and often win—though if she loses she may pay with her life.

FISHING BEAR

In Alaska, and Kamchatka in the Russian far east, brown bears have become expert at catching salmon as they migrate up rivers to spawn. The cubs learn their skills from the adults, pouncing on the fish in the shallows or seizing them in mid-air as they attempt to leap up waterfalls.

SECURE HOME

The beavers' home, or lodge, is built from branches and mud, and surrounded by the water of a pond created by damming a stream. It has an underwater entrance that leads to a dry chamber above the water level. This is where the kits rest and sleep with the family, safe from predators.

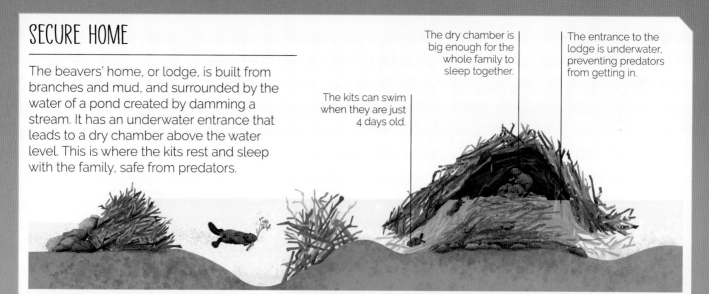

The dry chamber is big enough for the whole family to sleep together.

The entrance to the lodge is underwater, preventing predators from getting in.

The kits can swim when they are just 4 days old.

BABY BEAVERS

Young beavers live in families made up of an adult male and female, older brothers and sisters, and newborn babies known as kits. The mother beaver usually has up to four kits each spring. They are born with teeth and full coats of fur, and with their eyes open. Baby beavers stay in the safety of the lodge for about a month. They feed on their mother's milk at first, but quickly start to take solid food.

The newborn are kept warm by their mother's body.

BEAVER

Baby beavers can see and swim soon after they are born

Beavers live in the world's northern forests, where they spend much of their time in the water, even living under the ice when their ponds freeze over in winter. They cut down trees with their big chisel-like teeth and use the logs to dam streams, creating ponds that protect their homes and young from wolves, bears, and other enemies. Baby beavers start exploring their new world with their parents within a few days of being born.

The mother cares for her young, feeding and playing with them while their father watches for danger.

LIFE IN THE POND

Beaver kits are well-equipped for life in the water. They have transparent membranes that protect their eyes like a pair of goggles, and closable ears and nostrils. They soon learn how to find their own food, and practice using their teeth to fell trees.

Chisel teeth
Beaver teeth are strong and sharp, and keep growing throughout a baby beaver's life as they are worn down by gnawing through tree bark and timber. When old enough, beavers eat the bark, along with water plants, and gather edible twigs to store under the ice in winter.

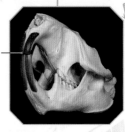

The front teeth are reinforced with iron, which tints them orange.

Scaly tail
A beaver can swim faster than you can walk, driving itself along using its webbed back feet and flattened, scaly tail. It also uses its tail to steer, and can warn other beavers of danger by slapping it loudly against the water.

FAMILY LIFE

Young beavers stay with their parents
for about two years, learning the skills
they need to build their own dams and
lodges when it's time to leave. Since
they are still living in the family home
when their mother has her next litter
of kits, the year-old young help out
by gathering food.

JAGUAR

The biggest cat of the American tropics

A jaguar cub will grow up to be the top predator in tropical American forests. From an early age, it learns how to kill by watching its mother—practicing first on small targets, such as squirrels. But by adulthood, it will have the strongest bite of any cat, with canine teeth that can puncture the hide of a crocodile.

The jaguar has the broken-ring (rosette) pattern of the related leopard—but differs by having spots in the middle of the rosettes.

CUB CARE

As in other cats, a jaguar cub develops a strong bond with its mom, who raises her offspring alone. On average, two cubs are born, but the forest is filled with danger and, despite her efforts, often only one survives. The cub suckles milk for up to six months, and for its entire first year rough play helps a cub learn how to defend itself and hunt for prey.

Every cub has its own **unique pattern** of spotted rosettes.

GROWING UP IN THE FOREST

The thick vegetation of the tropical forest means it is easy to hide under cover and ambush fast-moving prey, such as deer. However, cubs must develop plenty of skills just to get around in this complex habitat.

In the trees

Jaguars spend most of their time on the ground, but learning to climb brings a cub closer to tree-dwelling prey, including sloths, monkeys, and iguanas. Like other cats, they develop a good sense of balance, and strong, stocky legs with extendable claws help them to hold on.

Cubs first experience water by clinging to their mothers.

In the water

Jaguars live close to rivers and lakes, and often wait in ambush for prey at waterholes or along river banks. Splashing around in water makes a cub an expert swimmer—for cooling off in the tropical heat or catching more aquatic prey such as turtles, caimans, and crocodiles.

LIFE IN A POUCH

Like other marsupials, such as kangaroos, a koala is born at a very underdeveloped stage, after a short pregnancy of just over a month. The rest of its early development happens in the protection of the mother's pouch, where it grows quickly with its mother's nourishing milk.

Newborn

A newborn koala—blind, hairless, and no bigger than a jellybean—is little more than a body, head, and arms. It uses its arms to crawl to the mother's teat inside the pouch, where it will feed on milk until it is ready to emerge.

A baby peers out at the world, but stays inside the pouch until its limbs are strong enough to ride piggyback.

Getting bigger

The opening of a koala's pouch points downward, but a strong muscle works like a drawstring to stop the baby falling out. As the baby gets older, it starts to eat special green, jellylike droppings called pap, which are produced by its mother. This supplies its gut with microbes that will help with digestion when the young koala moves on to solid eucalyptus leaves.

KOALA

A marsupial that spends all its time eating and sleeping

For a baby koala, growing up in the forests of Australia means being carried by a tree-climbing mom—first in her marsupial pouch and then riding piggyback. For a while, the baby will return to the pouch for milk, but as its teeth grow it must prepare for a lifetime of eating tough eucalyptus leaves.

Sleepyheads
Young koalas begin to forage for eucalyptus leaves at about seven months old. These leaves are very tough and contain bitter chemicals and oils. It takes a long time to digest the leaves. Koalas manage by spending around two-thirds of their time—day and night—sleeping while their guts work on the food; most of their waking time is spent on browsing and chewing more leaves.

A koala's coat of fur is one of the thickest of any marsupial, and also provides the perfect protection from the cold, wind, and rain.

KOALA CARRIER

The same clawed feet that are so helpful for grasping branches and holding eucalyptus stems are used by a baby koala to cling tightly to its mom, with its head pressed close to hers. From around six months old, the baby spends more and more time out of the pouch. Then it will start to venture out onto the branches alone, but always within reach of mom.

LEARNING TO HUNT

Like other cats, bobcats are armed with two kinds of weapons—claws and teeth—and kittens learn how to use them most effectively. Claws are perfect for grabbing prey, while a bite to the back of the head quickly kills small prey. But growing bobcats learn that tackling bigger targets, such as deer, need a different hunting technique—a bite to the neck that suffocates the victim.

Claws
It's not long before bobcat kittens are climbing trees, using the four hooked claws on each paw to grip.

The claws can be drawn in when not needed.

Hunters
Bobcat kittens accompany their mother to seek out small rodents, hares, or rabbits at the age of three months. They are soon adept at ambushing small prey.

BOBCAT

Most bobcats are born into litters of two to four kittens

Bobcat kittens are born with tufted ears and a short, bobbed tail—features that show they belong to a group of cats called lynxes. They thrive in the forests of North America, where they become top predators, eventually learning to kill animals up to the size of deer.

EARLY DAYS

With plenty of prey around, a mother bobcat can produce two litters a year. Like most other cats, she raises her kittens alone. After giving birth in a rocky den that she lines with soft leaves, she leads them out into the world when they are around four months old. In just one or two years they will be old enough to have babies of their own.

Bobcats have a lifespan of about **10 years** in the wild.

Bobcats that live in cold northern forests develop thicker coats than those that live in warmer habitats farther south.

Long, dark hairs growing from the tip of the ears form a prominent tuft.

EARLY LIFE

Infants are carried on their mother's front for the first month. They then learn how to cling onto their mother's back, which can be precarious. They are soon confidently moving about alone and picking things up, though they will catch a ride on mom's back frequently in their first year. As they mature, females stay in the group into which they were born, while males move out.

A macaque's red face indicates a more dominant social position within the troop.

One infant is born to a macaque mom every other year. They are born in the spring.

MACAQUE

Baby macaques have to adapt to subzero temperatures

In southern Japan, macaques live in warm forests, but farther north they cope with lower temperatures. In places high in the mountains, where they are called snow monkeys, they survive the bitter winter snows by bathing in thermal pools. Young macaques are born into troops of around 40 individuals. They are mostly cared for by their mothers until they are about 18 months old.

In the winter, the coat grows far thicker to keep the macaque warm—the summer coat is lighter in weight.

Macaques cope with temperatures as low as **-4°F** (-20°C).

Time with mom
Macaques spend almost a third of their time ensuring their coats are clean of dirt and wingless insects called lice by combing through each other's fur. Grooming is also an important way for the macaques to maintain bonds within a troop. It is taught by the mothers to their infants.

FAST LEARNERS

Young macaques develop their skills quickly. By about four months, they can climb, leap, and forage for themselves.

Challenging leaps
Macaques spend time in trees as well as on the ground and the infants are soon adept at performing fearless leaps from tree to tree. They love to turn this into a game of chase.

Finding food
Baby macaques discover what to eat by watching and copying their mothers, and on one Japanese island they have learned to wash food, such as sweet potatoes, in water at the beach.

Playtime
Macaques are sociable animals and infants in particular like to play a lot, which helps them bond with others. Some macaques have even learned to make snowballs just for fun.

A HOT BATH

Japanese macaques are intelligent
animals, ready to learn from birth.
A troop living in freezing Jigokudani,
Japan, have learned to bathe in natural
hot springs in the winter, which helps
keep them warm. Young macaques
are quick to pick up such behavior
by watching the grown ups.

LEOPARD

A leopard cub stays close to its mother for the first two years of its life

Life for a leopard cub begins in the rocky cave where it was born, before it moves up in the world—leopards spend more time in trees than other big cats, and cubs soon learn to climb for safety. They have a devoted mother, but she must now spend more time away hunting for meat—sometimes leaving them alone for several days at a time.

Like all cats, the young are groomed by the mother licking their coats to clean them.

Whiskers

Cats have whiskers on their cheeks, muzzle, and above their eyes. These specialized hairs are rooted in skin sensors that are triggered by touch, and are especially well developed in nocturnal hunters such as leopards. As they move around, cubs instinctively extend their whiskers forward to help sense the world around them.

HIGH-RISE CAT

Although most other cats are not at home in a tree, a mother leopard and her cub are happy perched high. Unlike dogs, cats can rotate their paws, which is good for holding a branch as well as prey. Wide paws with extendable claws means that this cub has a secure grip while mom grooms and licks its fur. The leopard's coloring and pattern also provide it with the perfect camouflage among the trees or in the long grass.

LIFE LESSONS

Cubs stay with their mother for up to two years. During this time, they learn by watching and copying what she does, gaining skills along the way. It's an important time because once they leave the litter, they lead solitary lives.

Playing
Cubs are playful, often jumping on top of their mother and pouncing on each other. They begin to head out on hunting expeditions with their mom by about three months of age, so play like this is important because it strengthens their limbs and the accuracy of their pounces.

Prey
Once caught, prey is often dragged up into a tree to store it and keep it away from scavengers. Cubs develop their permanent canine teeth, which they use for stabbing prey, at about seven or eight months old. This is when they can start to kill small animals. Until then, they enjoy the meat on bigger kills supplied by their mother.

ORANGUTAN

A baby orangutan lives with its mom for about eight years

Orangutans are found in the rainforests of Borneo and Sumatra in Asia. The mother gives birth around once every eight years to a baby that weighs about 3 lb (1.5 kg)—human babies weigh, on average, more than twice as much. The baby is born in a tree and will spend most of its life in a tree. Its first instinct is to cling tightly to its mother, who is responsible for looking after it for the next seven or eight years.

Birth takes place on a nest **high** in the branches.

The mother makes herself a leaf pillow, while the baby uses mom as a pillow.

Nests are used for night sleeping, but an orangutan may retreat to its nest for a daytime rest.

A comfortable bed
Just like a human baby, an orangutan baby settles down at night in a specially made bed. Orangutans build sleeping platforms, weaving branches and leaves together to form a safe, sturdy nest. It takes about 10 minutes for the mother to build the platform, with the baby watching and learning how it's done—by the time it is three years old, it can build its own sleeping bed.

Hanging around
Orangutans are confident in their treetop homes well before they reach their first birthday. They have particularly long arms to help them swing—like its mom, a baby's arm span is longer than its body length. Mom and baby use long vines, called lianas, to help them move about.

BABY LIFE

Orangutan babies show great similarities to human babies. They respond eagerly to their mother's cuddles, they cry, and they show emotions such as surprise and fear. Orangutans don't live in groups, so all care is up to the mom.

The babies learn to lick tree sap, which is a nutrient-rich fluid produced by trees.

NATURE'S UMBRELLA

Orangutans appear to hate their fur getting wet—like humans using umbrellas, they will use large forest leaves for shelter. They pick up this handy trick by closely watching their mom and copying her behavior. The larger the leaf, the better!

ZEBRA

A zebra foal can stand within 20 minutes of its birth and run within the hour

Zebra foals are born on open grasslands and face an immediate battle to survive and reach adulthood. However, they have incredibly good senses—they see and hear well, and are particularly alert to danger. They are also born with legs almost as long as their mother's, and they are soon running at her side.

Life for the newborn

A foal is born after about a year of pregnancy and usually at night when there may be fewer predators. Standing up is initially hard and the newborn needs to spread its legs widely to do so. After that, it spends a short while alone with its mother, and the two begin the start of what will be a close bond. It soon becomes a part of a small group, consisting of a number of females, their young, and a dominant male, a stallion.

A UNIQUE PATTERN

Zebras in a herd may look identical, but all zebras have different patterns of stripes and, in the same way, a baby zebra's stripe pattern will be slightly different from its mother's. Some scientists think they are born with these stripes as an aid against biting insects—they act as an effective insect repellent.

A foal is born with **brown stripes** that turn black with age.

Running to survive

Lions focus on herd members that are easier to catch, so they will target the old or sick, and also the very young. A fully grown adult zebra can sometimes kick off an individual lion, but a foal has no chance, especially if it is separated from its herd. Many zebra foals are lost to lions.

The ears twist around to pinpoint the source of a sound, alerting the zebra to any danger.

SLOTH

A baby sloth is born in the treetops

Sloths live in the rainforests of Central and South America and spend their time in the tree canopy. Baby sloths cling tightly to their mother and rarely become separated but, if they do, they bleat loudly until found. Their cries are a lower pitch than most of the bird calls in the forest, which helps mom locate them. By the time they grow older, the only sound an adult sloth makes is a softer hiss.

A sloth's **first experience** is of its mother licking it clean.

Slow world

Sloths are the slowest mammals in the world, and spend at least 10 hours a day sleeping. Their claws and limbs lock into place while they sleep, which prevents them from tumbling out of their treetop home. A baby two-toed sloth sleeps nestled onto its mother's tummy. It will stay near its mom for about a year and sometimes more. The newborn relies on its mom to teach it how to survive in the treetops and even samples food from its mother's mouth when it is about a week old.

Leafy diet

Baby two-toed sloths drink their mother's milk for up to a year, but after the first week they also start feeding on leaves—their main diet. They are born with teeth and use their two front teeth to bite, while the others are flat and used to grind the leaves into a pulp. Their leafy diet is not very nutritious, so they sleep a lot to save energy.

UPSIDE DOWN

A baby sloth spends its first six months clinging to mom, before beginning to explore a little farther. Sloths move through the trees upside down, so a baby has a safe perch on its mother's tummy. She is partly camouflaged from predators by her slow movements as well as by the green algae that grows in her hair, and will defend her baby with her long, sharp claws.

Baby sloths can have pale or dark brown hair, depending upon geographic location.

GAINING INDEPENDENCE

This baby two-toed sloth has been rescued from the forest floor and is in a sanctuary, where it will be cared for until it can be released back into the wild. Baby sloths need nursing several times a day. They can hang upside down when they are about 20 days old, and are bold enough to explore when they are seven weeks old.

LIFE UNDERWATER

There are many advantages to living underwater. Baby hippos use the water to ensure their sensitive skin remains moist and healthy. They also use lakes and rivers to avoid the intense African heat and the threat of predators on land.

Walk or swim?
Baby hippos soon feel at home in the water. Like adults, calves can't swim so they walk along river beds or lake floors using their weight to stop them from floating upward. They also feast on aquatic plants from about the age of three weeks old.

Hippo school
Mothers allow their babies to join larger groups of family and friends when they are a few months old. These noisy, sociable hippo schools create safety in numbers for up to 100 members, young and old.

WATER BABIES

Mother hippos give birth in the lakes and rivers of the African savanna, so their calves must paddle to the surface to breathe for the first time. Most of their lives are spent submerged in water. They feed on their mother's milk underwater until they are eight months old. At first, babies can only hold their breath for less than a minute, but by adulthood they can stay submerged for five minutes.

An oily red substance is released to protect the skin against sunburn.

HIPPO

Baby hippos are born underwater

A baby hippo stays with its mom for up to **8 years**.

Hippopotamuses are true heavyweights of the animal kingdom with huge heads, powerful bodies, and hefty legs. Their babies are born so big that most mothers can only give birth to one calf every two years. A newborn hippopotamus weighs about the same as a human teenager. They grow very quickly, reaching five times their birth weight within the first year.

The nostrils close when the hippo is submerged to stop water entering.

PARENTAL BOND

For 10 days after giving birth, a mother hippopotamus is fiercely defensive of her newborn—even chasing away her older offspring. But over time, family bonds are restored and a mother will often rest and wallow with two or even three of her calves—each of different ages.

AFRICAN WILD DOG

For African wild dogs, raising pups is all about cooperation

African wild dogs live in packs that have a strong bond—they hunt together, share food, and sleep nestled up to each other. The pups are welcomed into this sociable group and fiercely protected. Usually, only one pair will breed and produce young, and the larger the pack size, the better it is for raising cubs successfully—it means better hunting and more protection.

FOOD ON DEMAND

By eight weeks, the pups are completely weaned from milk and feed on meat. They grow up on regurgitated meat. Each adult can gulp down 9 lb (4 kg) of meat at a time and bring its full belly back to the den to feed the pups and even other adults, including the nursing mother who relies on this after she's given birth. But the pups soon learn to feed from a kill directly, and eventually join in the hunt.

The biggest packs have more than 30 dogs.

Big litter
Group care means that African wild dogs can raise big litters: on average 10 pups are born at a time, but 21 have been recorded. After spending three months in an underground den, they emerge into the protection of the pack. While some adults are out hunting for meat, other dogs stay behind to babysit the brood and chase away predators.

Safety in the den
When danger threatens, the pups return to the safety of the den where they were born, which is often the empty burrow of an aardvark, porcupine, or warthog. They will use the den for refuge and shelter there until they are 16 weeks old.

The huge ears give the African wild dog an acute sense of hearing. They also help keep it cool by shedding excess body heat.

The Latin name for African wild dog means "painted wolf" and refers to its patterned coat.

PLAYTIME

Like many mammals, young African wild dogs love to play, and large litters mean they get plenty of opportunity to do so. Unlike many mammals, adults will often continue this behavior. Play is important to social animals such as African wild dogs because it helps the pack maintain a close bond.

LIFE AS A CHIMP

Like us, chimps have opposable thumbs, which means they can use their hands to grip things. They also have opposable big toes (humans don't). This means they can use both their hands and feet to help them in their everyday lives, performing all sorts of tasks.

Keeping clean

Chimpanzees groom each other by spreading the fur with their hands and picking out dirt and insects with their fingers or mouths. Grooming is important to chimps as it strengthens the bonds, helps relax them, and keeps their coats clear of insects that may cause illness. A mother will regularly groom her offspring.

Agile animals

Chimps spend a lot of their time up in trees. Very young chimps soon show how comfortable they are in that habitat, quickly gaining confidence in life many feet above the ground. They have incredibly strong arms and legs, and a tight grip with their hands and feet means they can easily and quickly swing through the treetops.

CHIMPANZEE

Young chimpanzees are totally dependent on their mother for the first five years of their life

Chimpanzees, our close relatives, live in communities of up to 120 individuals, and the young are cared for by their mothers for around five years. For the first month or so, a baby will hang on to its mother's belly. After that it often rides on her back.

Chimps communicate to others in their group with loud calls known as pant-hoots.

Using tools
Chimpanzees spend a lot of time during the day foraging for food, using sticks and stones as tools. Young chimpanzees learn how to do this by watching and copying older members of their group. They use twigs to fish out termites and ants or to extract honey from a bee's nest. They also use stones for cracking nuts and scrunched up leaves as sponges to collect water.

Young chimpanzees poke twigs into holes in a termite nest to scoop up their favorite food—but it takes a lot of practice to perfect the technique.

LEARNING FROM MOM

Chimpanzees are similar to humans in many ways. Just like us, baby chimps cry, show fear or excitement, smile, and even laugh. They use a lot of sounds to communicate, as well as facial expressions and gestures such as hugging. A young chimp soon learns to respond to its mother's calls as well as beginning to interact with others in the group.

Infant chimps have faces that are much paler than those of the adults.

Female chimps can produce up to **nine babies** in their lifetime.

HARDY CALF

Reindeer have adapted to live in three types of habitat—Arctic, tundra, and woodland. Calves reared farthest north must cope with the coldest conditions. But they are physically tough, and can even regulate their body temperature straight after birth.

Blending in

Calves are born in May or June, when the ground has a covering of summer growth. They tend to hide from predators in undergrowth for the first few days when they need frequent rests. Their brown coat helps them blend in with their habitat, making it harder for predators to spot. In winter, the coat turns a lighter, whitish-gray and this helps them blend in with their snowy environment.

Keeping warm

Every part of a calf's body is covered in hairs, including the soles of its hooves, so it doesn't feel the cold. By the first winter, it has put on extra fat and has grown a thick, layered coat, which is much thicker than its parents'. The outer, woolly layer has hollow hairs that insulate the calf to keep it warm, and help the calf stay afloat when swimming across rivers. The thicker underfur traps air, stopping body heat from escaping.

REINDEER

Reindeer calves double their weight in their first two weeks

Reindeer, known as caribou in North America, roam Alaska, northern Canada, Greenland, and Siberia. A newborn reindeer is small and very vulnerable to attack from wolves, golden eagles, and bears. It needs to be able to move along with the herd quickly, but the calf struggles to get onto its feet at first. Encouraged by its mother, who licks her newborn and fluffs up its fur, it is up and ready to move within a few hours.

Growing up

The newborn calf feeds on its mother's milk for the first month of life before beginning to graze on grass, leaves, and lichen. The milk is incredibly rich—four times as nutritious as a cow's milk—and helps the calf's rapid growth. The mother is responsible for her newborn, but being in a herd also gives the baby protection from predators.

Hair on the sole of the hooves helps the calf grip ice.

STAYING CLOSE

Most female reindeer usually give birth to one calf. They stick close to their mother for the first couple of months, but as they get stronger and older, they venture farther away. Keeping up with mom and the herd means occasionally reaching speeds of almost 50 mph (80 kph).

SUMMER MIGRATION

Some reindeer populations migrate thousands of miles in the summer in search of new feeding grounds. The calves follow their mothers, even crossing rivers—they can swim faster than most people can walk. Wide hooves also help the young paddle through the water.

IN THE POUCH

A opossum usually has six to ten tiny young. They are born when they are only half-developed, but they are able to use their arms to haul themselves into their mother's pouch. Here, they stay safe while they grow into furry baby opossums.

Playing dead

If it senses danger, often from an animal that hunts live prey, this young opossum has a surprising way of defending itself. It rolls over and lies limp and still, with its eyes open and tongue hanging out, releasing a nasty smell as if dead. This is usually enough to make its enemy leave it alone.

Tiny babies

At birth the bee-size young are naked, blind, and almost helpless, but they are able to find their way through their mother's fur and into her pouch. Once inside, they feed on their mother's milk for the next eight weeks, with the milk providing all they need to complete their development.

Baby opossums cling tightly to their mother's fur to stay safe.

Overcrowded

After eight weeks the babies relax their grip on their milk supply, but return to it whenever they are hungry. Altogether they stay in the pouch for up to 11 weeks. As they grow, they take up more and more room in the pouch. Eventually, it becomes too crowded, and the now well-developed young climb out and onto their mother's back.

A mother opossum can have as many as **21 babies** at a time.

OPOSSUM

Baby opossums use their mother as a taxi service

The Virginia opossum is a marsupial, whose babies develop in a pouch on their mother's belly until they are old enough to hitch a ride on her back. Most marsupials live in Australia and South America, but the Virginia opossum has spread over much of the US and as far north as Canada. Opossums will eat almost anything they can find, and they often turn up in backyards—complete with babies—in search of food.

FREE RIDE

The mother opossum carries her family on her back wherever she goes—even up trees. As time goes on, they learn the lessons they need to survive. Following their mother's example they start eating solid food, and finally leave when they are four or five months old to fend for themselves.

When climbing, a opossum uses its tail to grip branches.

HANGING AROUND

Like their mother, baby opossums have strong, prehensile tails, which they can wrap around branches to help them climb. But unlike her, they are very light, so their tails can easily support their weight. They could dangle like this for hours, but they will soon think of a better game!

INSEPARABLE

A mother rhinoceros is devoted to her baby and the pair are inseparable. The newborn nurses on its mother's milk for up to 18 months, with male calves suckling more often and longer than female ones, which helps them grow much bigger than females. The mother keeps her offspring safe against attacks by crocodiles and lions. Spending time alongside its mother teaches the baby where to find good grazing and water supplies, as well as how to escape predators. When the rhinoceros is two years old, it has both the size and skills to fend for itself in the wild.

A rhino's skin is thick, but they can still suffer sunburn.

RHINOCEROS

Baby rhinoceroses are born without horns

Among the world's heaviest creatures, this powerhouse of the African savanna is born big. Newborn rhinoceroses weigh the same as the average 12-year-old human. To maximize their chances of survival, they stand up and walk within days of being born. They stay by their mother's side for her milk and protection until they reach adulthood.

The horns of a rhino never stop growing. They are used for digging and for protecting the calves from predators.

GRASSLAND GRAZERS

Rhinoceroses spend most of the time grazing on the grasslands. They also socialize in family groups and cool off by rolling in mud.

Female families
Mother rhinoceroses and their babies sometimes form larger groups with other cows and calves. These groups are called crashes. Males usually live alone in their own territories.

Bird benefits
Rhinoceroses have niggling ticks and parasites on their skin. Oxpeckers pick them off to eat and in turn help keep the rhinoceroses' skin healthy. The birds also act as an early warning system, flying off when predators approach.

Mud bath
Calves cannot sweat so they keep cool by wallowing in mud. This provides a protective layer to stop the intense heat burning their skin and prevent insect bites.

GUANACO

Guanaco babies can stand just minutes after birth

A baby guanaco is known as a chulengo. It is born into a herd of around seven or more females, a single adult male, and other young. Guanacos—relatives of llamas and camels—live in open habitats of South America, from deserts to windy plains. They tend to stick to open grassland and avoid the steep mountain slopes. It can be a tough environment for the chulengos.

NEW ARRIVAL

Guanacos give birth between December and February, depending on where they live. These are the summer months in the southern hemisphere, when food is usually plentiful, so the chulengos have time to put on weight for the winter. The birthing process is a vulnerable time for the herd, and they are adapted to make it as quick as possible.

Giving birth
A guanaco's pregnancy lasts about a year. The mother gives birth standing up on open grassland. Like other members of the camel family, the mother's tongue is too short to lick her baby. But, because the birth takes place in the midday heat, the sun dries out the baby's coat.

Standing up
The chulengo struggles to its feet soon after birth and can usually walk within the first hour. It begins to seek out its mother's milk less than an hour after birth and will continue to be nursed by its mother until it is about eight months old.

Like all members of the camel family, guanacos have a split upper lip. They use this to reach for and grasp food.

WELCOME TO THE HERD!

Smell is important to guanacos and a chulengo is sniffed by herd members to cement its acceptance into the group. The young are born within the space of a few days and are soon gathering together to play, leaping confidently over the bumpy ground on which they live.

ON GUARD!

Guanacos are hunted by pumas (also known as mountain lions), and the young learn to stay as alert to danger as the adults. If a member of a herd spots something unusual, they sound a high-pitched call as a warning to get ready to run.

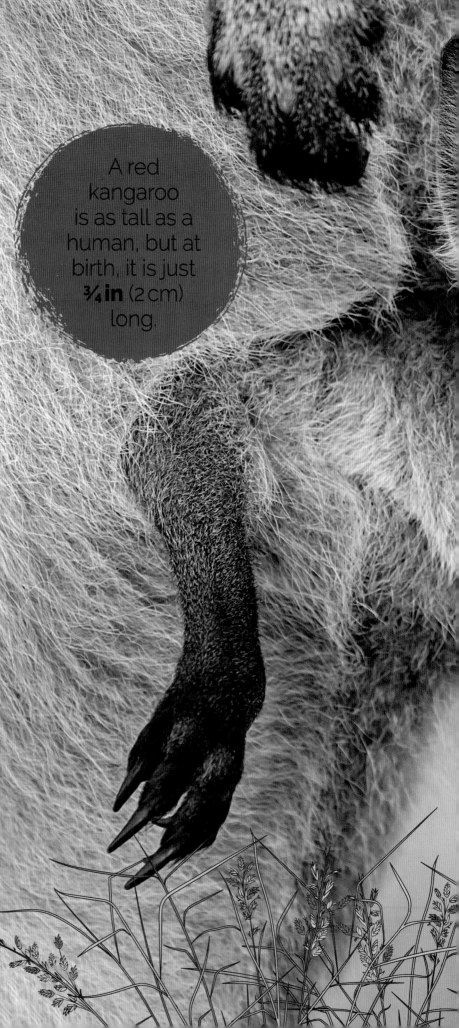

SAFE REFUGE

A baby red kangaroo is born after a very short pregnancy of just 36 days. Most of its development takes place while it is in its mother's pouch.

Tiny but not helpless
At birth the joey is like an animated jelly bean—blind, deaf, naked, and with no back legs. But it can use its arms to crawl toward the pouch, along a path that its mother licks through her fur.

Inside the pouch
When it gets into the pouch, the joey latches onto a teat and starts drinking. Its mother's milk contains all it needs to grow into a well-developed baby.

Getting bigger
The joey stays attached to its milk supply for up to five months. After that it lets go, and only feeds when it is hungry. But it stays in the pouch for another few weeks until it feels it is safe to emerge.

A red kangaroo is as tall as a human, but at birth, it is just **¾ in** (2 cm) long.

KANGAROO

A joey grows up inside its mother's pouch

Kangaroos are marsupials—mammals that give birth to tiny, half-formed young and carry them in a pouch until they are able to survive in the outside world. Even after leaving the pouch, a baby kangaroo—known as a joey— is always ready to climb back in at the slightest hint of danger, or just to feed on its mother's rich milk.

The joey's big eyes and ears are alert to everything.

MOBILE HOME

Safe in its mother's pouch, this baby kangaroo is carried everywhere she goes. The pouch even tightens up when she is hopping along at speed to make sure it doesn't fall out. When it is old enough, the joey pokes its head out and starts taking an interest in its surroundings. Eventually, it climbs out of the pouch for the first time, but soon hops back in.

The mouth and teeth are adapted for gathering plant foods.

A young kangaroo's face gets longer as it grows.

Growing up
As the joey gets older, it gets used to its mother calling it back into the pouch whenever she senses a threat. But when this kangaroo mother is about to have another baby she stops letting the first one climb into her pouch. The young kangaroo still relies on its mother's milk, but gradually it learns to eat grass, leaves, and other solid foods.

IBEX

An ibex must learn to trust its climbing instincts within two weeks of being born

An ibex is a type of wild goat, legendary for its ability to clamber up steep cliffs. As its feet are specially adapted to grip the rock, it has no fear of heights. It confidently leaps from crag to crag in places where a slip could plunge it to certain death on the rocks below. Baby ibex—known as kids—are as fearless as their parents, ready to follow them up onto the highest, narrowest rocky ledges when only a few days old.

A Nubian ibex can live up to **16 years** in the wild.

SPECIAL EQUIPMENT

Like other wild goats, ibex have two toes on each hoof that spread out to grip the ground. The toes have rubbery soles, and the sharp edges of the hooves are strong enough to bear the ibex's weight when slotted into narrow gaps.

The outer wall is strengthened with keratin.

The toes spread out for extra grip.

The soft sole acts like a suction pad.

Rubbery sole pad

SIDE VIEW OF HOOF

HOOF FROM BELOW

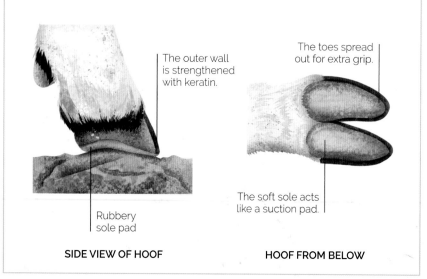

Battling it out
Adult males use their spectacular horns to fight each other over females, and young ibex at play mimic their combat. These play fights often take place on dangerous terrain, but accidents are rare.

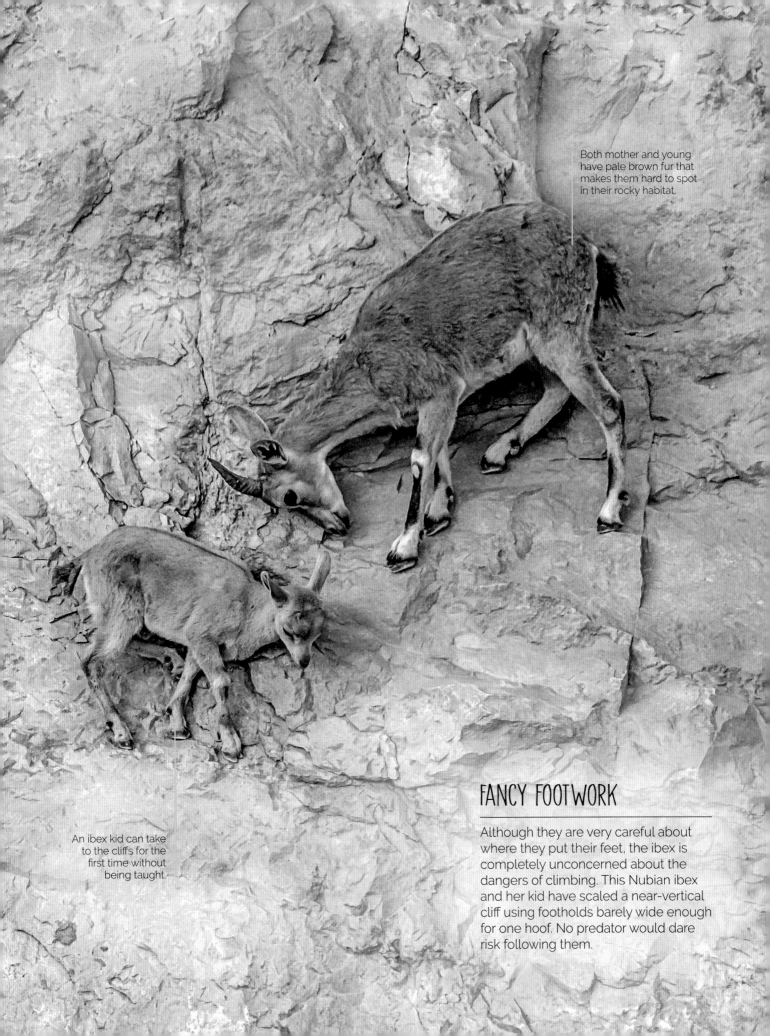

Both mother and young have pale brown fur that makes them hard to spot in their rocky habitat.

An ibex kid can take to the cliffs for the first time without being taught.

FANCY FOOTWORK

Although they are very careful about where they put their feet, the ibex is completely unconcerned about the dangers of climbing. This Nubian ibex and her kid have scaled a near-vertical cliff using footholds barely wide enough for one hoof. No predator would dare risk following them.

PROUD PARENT

A female ibex usually has one kid at a time, but many have twins. At first she feeds them on her milk, until they start nibbling on leaves as well. Newborn kids have no horns, but they soon start to grow, and keep growing throughout life. An adult male's horns can be up to 50 in (127 cm) long.

HUMPBACK WHALE

A baby whale is nursed underwater by its mother

A humpback whale calf is already the length of a small car at birth. It is born tail first, underwater, and depends on the mother's milk and protection for survival. The whale mother nudges her baby to the surface to take a first breath, and the calf is soon drinking more than 9 gallons (40 liters) of milk a day. In the first year, the calf will double in length.

Acrobatic whales
Humpback whales often leap out of the water. This is known as breaching. Calves pick up this behavior at a young age. Why they do this is unclear—it may be a form of communication or may help them clear their skin of parasites. It's also possible they are having fun!

STAYING CLOSE

A calf stays close to its mother, with both frequently touching. About three months after birth, they set off on a journey—humpback whales migrate, spending winters close to the equator, where they give birth, and summers in polar waters, which are rich in food. On their journey, mother and calf communicate in whispers, using a series of chirrups and squeaks. Scientists think this helps them avoid being detected by predators.

Taking a breath
Humpbacks have to breathe air—they are mammals and have lungs like humans. Their nostrils, known as blowholes, are on top of their heads. Once they take a breath, they dive down and can remain under the water for several minutes.

The calf swims close to its mother until it becomes a confident swimmer.

A whale calf keeps growing until it is about **50 ft** (16 m) in length.

Once a mother and calf become tired, the killer whales move in to attack.

Dangerous seas
A mother and her calf are vulnerable to attack from killer whales (also known as orcas) during their long migration. Killer whales work in teams, targeting a youngster and aiming to separate the mother from her calf.

MANATEE

A grazing mammal that lives underwater

Manatees are distant cousins of elephants, but thick, bare skin and a vegetarian diet seem to be the only things they have in common. This is because manatees are adapted to be aquatic. A baby manatee is born underwater and stays there for the rest of its life, in warm shallows off tropical coastlines, where thick plant growth provides good grazing for growing up.

A newborn manatee calf weighs up to **66 lb** (30 kg).

Nostrils are high on the muzzle, which helps the manatee breathe easily when it comes to the surface.

LONG PARTNERSHIP

A calf stays with its mother for up to two years to feed on her milk, keeping close enough to communicate with squeaks, grunts, and moans. The mother's teats are in the "armpits" of her flippers, so the calf approaches her from behind when it wants to suckle.

Manatees have strong lips like snouts that help them eat.

The first moments
A manatee calf can rise to the surface independently to take its first breath. It has visible wrinkles on its skin called fetal folds. These are caused by being curled up inside its mom's womb, and take weeks to wear off.

A calf flexes its spoon-shaped tail, moving it up and down to glide in the water.

LIFE UNDERWATER

Manatees, like all mammals, have lungs, so they must come to the surface every two to four minutes to take a breath. Because they stick to shallow waters, they don't have to dive deeply, but can stay submerged while resting for up to 24 minutes.

Each flipper has four tiny nails.

Underwater resting
The dense, heavy bones of a manatee's skeleton means that it can easily sink to the bottom, where it can rest or sleep. Sometimes a manatee will lie upside down to scratch its back on rocks, helping it reach parts that the tiny nails on its flippers cannot reach.

Fields of grass
Manatees are often referred to as sea cows because they graze on underwater plants, such as seagrasses, mangrove leaves, and algae. The calves begin nibbling on underwater plants just a few weeks after birth, using their flexible upper lip (prehensile lip) to grasp stalks and manipulate them into their mouth.

SENSITIVE FACE

Like its mom, a manatee calf has thousands of tiny hairs all over its face. These give the manatee its amazing sense of touch. A calf will sometimes playfully prod its mom, but their unique sense of touch comes in handy when feeling their way through murky river water.

BIRDS

All baby birds hatch from eggs, but from that point their lives vary hugely. Some are blind, featherless, and almost helpless when they hatch, needing to be kept warm and fed by their parents. But others, like this ostrich chick, are up and about almost right away, and are even able to peck around and find their own food.

An adult flamingo develops its pink plumage over two or three years.

EARLY DAYS

When it hatches from the egg, a baby flamingo is covered with fluffy, gray down. It has a short pink bill and pink legs, but these soon turn black. After a few days, the chick leaves the nest and joins other young flamingos in a big flock guarded by adults, called a crèche. But the chick still relies on its parents for food until it is about ten weeks old and can feed itself.

Kept warm by its mother, this flamingo chick has a pink bill, which shows that it is less than a week old.

FLAMINGO

Flamingo chicks are born with gray feathers

Flamingos are amazingly long-legged, long-necked water birds that feed in the shallow waters of coastal lagoons and salty lakes, sifting tiny animals and plantlike algae from the water with their curved bills. But young flamingos cannot feed like this because their bills are the wrong shape. Instead, they are fed special "flamingo milk" by both their parents until they are old enough to take care of themselves.

Nesting site

All flamingos nest in dense colonies, usually on muddy islands just above water level. Some colonies of lesser flamingos on African lakes contain millions of birds. Each pair scrapes the mud into a mound with a hollow in the middle, where the female lays a single big, white egg. Both parents then take turns sitting on the egg for about a month to keep it warm until it hatches.

The nest is raised about 12 in (30 cm) above the surrounding mud to protect the egg and chick from flooding.

PINK DIET

A flamingo gets its colorful plumage from its food. It eats tiny, floating algae or small animals that feed on the algae. Pigments in the algae get into the bird's blood, travel to its skin, and are built into its feathers.

Flamingo milk

Until their chick is old enough to find its own food, both parents feed it with a pink, protein-rich fluid made in their foodpipes called crop milk. Flamingos, pigeons, and male emperor penguins are the only birds that can do this.

Filter feeding

As a young flamingo grows, its bill changes shape and becomes lined with comblike fringes. With its bill upside-down, it forces water through the fringes with its powerful tongue to trap tiny animals and algae.

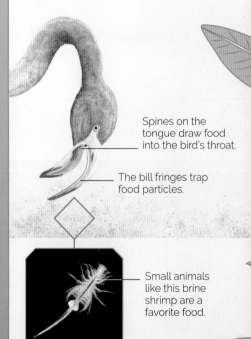

Spines on the tongue draw food into the bird's throat.

The bill fringes trap food particles.

Small animals like this brine shrimp are a favorite food.

FLAMINGO CRÈCHE

When these baby flamingos leave their nests they gather in flocks beneath the feet of watchful adults. Still too young to strain their own food from the water, they are fed by their parents. Somehow the parents recognize their own young by their calls, ignoring all the others.

GREBE

The striped chicks of great crested grebes enjoy a free ride

Grebes are sleek water birds that breed on freshwater lakes and marshes in summer, often migrating to coastal waters in winter. The great crested grebe is an elegant bird, with striking tufts of feathers on its head that form a flamboyant crest when the bird is excited. Its chicks are active as soon as they hatch, and soon leave the waterside nest. But rather than take their chances on the water they ride on the backs of their parents until they are able to swim, dive, and find food for themselves.

Great crested grebe chicks have distinctive black and white stripes along their heads and necks.

LAKESIDE NURSERY

A grebe's legs are located near the back of its body, which is perfect for swimming and diving, but makes walking very awkward. To avoid having to struggle on land, breeding pairs nest on the edges of lakes so they can slip into the water easily.

Floating home
Great crested grebes build a nesting platform of waterweed on the edge of the water—or even floating on it, anchored to plants such as reeds. The female lays four eggs, and the pair take turns to incubate them. If danger threatens, the birds may slip away to safety on the water, but not before carefully covering the eggs with waterweed to conceal them.

The eggs hatch in order of being laid.

Hatching out
After four weeks the chicks are ready to hatch. One by one, each baby grebe chips its way out of the egg, emerging covered with fluffy down feathers and with its eyes open. The chicks are active right away, and within a few hours they are able to leave the nest, following their parents out onto the water where they are safe from foxes and other land predators.

RIDING HIGH

Once they are on the water, the adults carry the chicks on their backs. This keeps the young birds warm, and also protects them from hunters that might attack from below, such as hungry pike. The parents usually split the brood between them, carrying two chicks each, but as they grow more confident the chicks start experimenting with swimming on their own.

The chicks ride on the backs of their parents for weeks, except when learning to swim.

PENGUIN

Emperor penguin chicks start life in the most hostile habitat on Earth

To be sure that their chicks grow up during the short Antarctic summer, emperor penguins must lay and incubate their eggs during the previous winter. They are forced to do this in the coldest, most extreme habitat endured by any bird— the frozen wastes of the Antarctic sea ice.

Guarding the egg

Emperor penguins gather to breed on sea ice lying close to the shore. Each female lays a single egg, and passes it to the male to incubate for about 64 days while she goes away to feed at sea. He holds the egg on his feet to stop it touching the ice, covering it with a fold of skin to keep it warm.

Although covered with fluffy down feathers, a chick still needs to snuggle into the adult's warm belly feathers to keep out the bitter Antarctic chill.

The chicks can be noisy, but so can the parents, who recognize their chick's call and respond with their own distinctive call.

PRECIOUS CHICKS

During their long vigil incubating the eggs, the males cannot eat. They huddle together, taking turns on the inside of the huddle where it is warmest. Finally, the chicks hatch, so their fathers have to keep them warm, too. They also feed the chicks with a nutritious fluid called crop milk, produced from each male's own throat.

Feeding time
When the chick is a few days old its mother comes back from the open sea, trekking up to 125 miles (200 km) over the ice to bring food for the hungry chick. This allows the male to go to sea to find food for himself, after going without any at all for up to four months.

An emperor penguin colony can contain more than **5,000 birds**.

The loose, feathery belly skin of the adult forms a snug pouch for the chick.

For eight weeks the parents take turns to carry the chick on their feet.

LIFE IN THE COLD

Although the sea ice is not as cold as the heart of Antarctica, the average air temperature is still a bone-chilling -4°F (-20°C) in winter. The penguins and their chicks are kept warm by a combination of closely packed feathers and a thick layer of fat.

First feathers
After their first few weeks relying on their parents for warmth, the chicks grow thick coats of gray down feathers. These trap a layer of warm air near the skin, helping keep out the freezing winds that sweep off the Antarctic ice sheets. Later, they lose the gray down, replacing it with oily, waterproof, black and white feathers adapted for swimming.

First swim
When the sea ice starts to break up in summer, the chicks make their first attempts at swimming and diving. Before long they are streaking through the water like torpedoes, driving themselves along with their wings and using their feet to steer. They soon learn to catch their own prey, diving deep below the surface to find fish, squid, and shrimplike krill.

GROUP HUG

When emperor penguin chicks are about two months old they gather in tight groups, huddling together to share their warmth and keep out the worst of the weather. They may have to endure blizzards driven by icy winds blowing at hurricane force.

Most cuckoos feed on insect prey, including crickets and caterpillars.

The adult bird must work hard to satisfy the cuckoo's big appetite.

Although almost fully grown, this young cuckoo still has the colorful mouth lining of a baby bird.

BIG BABY

A young cuckoo is always much bigger than its foster parents, and looks quite different. Despite this, they carry on feeding it, even when it has grown all its feathers and left the nest. Before long, this cuckoo will fly to Africa—amazingly they do this journey all alone without their parents to guide them.

A female cuckoo lays up to **23 eggs** in different nests.

ODD ONE OUT

Cunning cuckoo
By keeping careful watch, a female cuckoo locates the nest of a songbird, steals an egg, and lays one of her own eggs in its place. Her egg looks very like the others, but is slightly bigger. The adult songbirds do not notice, and incubate it along with their own.

Killer instinct
As soon as it hatches, the blind, naked baby cuckoo gets rid of the other eggs, removing all competition for food. It wriggles its body under each one so it sits in a hollow on its back, then carries it to the edge of the nest and leans back so the egg falls to the ground.

The young cuckoo weighs ten times as much as its foster parent.

CUCKOO

A baby cuckoo never knows its true parents

The common cuckoo is famous for the male's two-note song in spring. But it is also notorious for being a brood parasite—a bird that lays its eggs in the nests of songbirds and fools them into rearing its chicks. They do this even though the infant cuckoo destroys their own eggs and young.

No mercy
If any of the other songbird eggs have hatched, the helpless young get the same treatment. They are unable to stop the determined baby cuckoo forcing them onto its back and throwing them out of the nest. Ignored by their parents, they soon die.

Hungry chick
When the cuckoo has the nest to itself, it is able to eat all the food that the adult birds would bring to feed an entire family of four or more chicks. Driven by its begging calls, the foster parents stuff insect prey into its gaping, bright orange mouth.

BIG FAMILY

During the breeding season each male claims a territory with booming calls and displays. These attract several females who all lay their eggs in the same nest. As a result, the nest may contain up to 60 eggs.

Nesting site
One female stays with the eggs, along with the male. They take turns to incubate the eggs for six weeks, the female keeping them warm by day and the male by night. If space is tight the female may get rid of a few eggs, but only the ones laid by other females. When the chicks hatch, the adults keep close watch, using their wings to shade them from the midday sun.

Chasing predators
The male and dominant female are very attentive, defending their brood from any kind of threat. If they are approached by a hungry lion or hyena the male may pretend to be injured to distract the predator while the female leads the young away to safety. Even a harmless antelope will be seen off with a vigorous wing-flapping display.

OSTRICH

Baby ostriches look out for each other

The biggest of all birds, ostriches are flightless, with short wings and huge, fluffy down feathers instead of the sleek vanes of flying birds. They live on the dry grasslands of Africa, where each male usually mates with several females and then looks after their eggs and young.

Fluffy down feathers act like fur, keeping the ostrich chick warm.

STICKING TOGETHER

Ostrich chicks are active as soon as they hatch, and they are able to feed themselves. But they stick together for safety, keeping a lookout for enemies. When they feel they are safe, they peck around on the ground for seeds, insects, and anything else they can find to eat.

An ostrich egg is the **biggest** of any bird.

Big eyes with good vision detect any hint of danger.

OVERSHADOWED

Although an ostrich's egg is huge, it is very small compared to the bird that lays it. This means that while newly hatched ostriches are much bigger than most chicks, they are tiny compared to the adults. Here, a chick standing in the water is dwarfed by its huge parent.

VITAL WATER

Every day, often at dawn, sandgrouse fly across the desert in search of pools of water, gathering to drink in flocks of hundreds or even thousands. During the breeding season, the males do not just satisfy their own thirst, but collect water to take back to their chicks.

Flying sponge

The chicks cannot fly long distances until they are two months old, so they rely on their father to supply them with water. Wading belly-deep into the water, keeping his wings and tail clear, he rocks his body to and fro. This gathers water into his belly feathers, which are specially adapted to hold it like a sponge.

A thirsty chick sips water from its father's feathers.

Safe delivery

When the male sandgrouse has soaked up enough water, he takes off and flies back to the nesting site. On his return, he stands over each chick, raising his body upright so the water drains from the feathery sponge and into a central groove on his belly. This makes it easy for the chick to drink all the water it needs.

SANDGROUSE

Baby sandgrouse need their fathers to keep them supplied with vital water

Sandgrouse are partridge-like relatives of doves that live in flocks in the deserts and dry scrublands of Africa, Asia, and Spain. They feed on small seeds that contain very little water, forcing the birds to make daily flights to waterholes to drink. But their chicks cannot fly, so during the breeding season the adult males gather water for them by soaking it up in their feathers, and carrying it back to the nesting site.

A sandgrouse may fly **50 miles** (80 km) to fetch water.

Lying low

Before the chicks learn to control their body temperature, their parents have to keep them warm at night and shade them from the midday sun. At other times, their camouflage makes them hard to see in the dry, dusty terrain, helping protect them from hawks and other predators. Despite this, many struggle to survive.

The chicks venture out of the nest as soon as their fluffy down feathers have dried out after hatching.

QUICK LEARNERS

Female sandgrouse usually lay three eggs in a nest on the ground. The chicks are active as soon as they hatch, and leave the nest to start pecking on seeds. Copying their mother, they quickly learn which seeds to eat and which to avoid. One parent always stays with them when the other flies away to find water.

KIWI

Kiwi chicks are ready to look for food soon after they hatch

Kiwis are flightless, almost wingless birds that evolved on islands with no land mammals except bats. This allowed them to live like mammals themselves, snuffling through the forests by night in search of worms and insects that—unusually for birds—they detect by scent. Young kiwis must learn these skills early in life, but many are now killed by cats, dogs, and other mammals introduced to their native New Zealand.

Fluffy feathers
Kiwi feathers do not have the tiny barbs that zip typical feathers into flat vanes. This makes the feathers fluffy and more like the fur of mammals, which is ideal for keeping the bird warm as it searches for food by night.

GIANT EGGS

A female kiwi is the size of a farmyard hen, but her egg is six times as big as a hen's egg, and can be almost a quarter of her body weight. She must eat three times as much as usual as the egg grows. Eventually, however, she cannot eat at all because it takes up so much space inside her. When she is ready, she lays the egg in a burrow, where the male incubates it until it hatches. The kiwi chick is born with all its feathers, and is just like a miniature version of its parents.

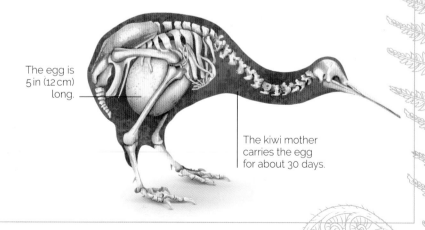

The egg is 5 in (12 cm) long.

The kiwi mother carries the egg for about 30 days.

Only about **5 percent** of kiwis survive to reach adulthood.

A kiwi's tiny, useless wings are buried invisibly in its body feathers.

Foraging for food
Probing the ground and tree crevices with its long bill, the kiwi soon learns how to find worms, burrowing beetle grubs, and other small animals. Its bill is sensitive to touch, and has a pair of nostrils near the tip for detecting the scent of prey. This enables it to sniff out a meal in the same way as a badger or fox. It cannot see very well, but this doesn't affect its ability to find food.

ACTIVE CHICK

A kiwi chick develops inside its outsize egg for up to three months before it hatches. This means it is very well equipped for life almost as soon as it emerges. The egg has an extra-large yolk that feeds the newly hatched chick for its first week, and after this it is able to find its own food on the forest floor.

The long, curved, sensitive bill is perfect for probing deep into soft ground.

OWL

Young great gray owls learn to hunt their prey in pitch darkness

With their big, forward-facing eyes surrounded by fans of stiff feathers, owls are unmistakable. The great gray owl is one of the biggest—a ghostly giant of the northern forests. Like most owls, it hunts by night for mice, voles, and other small animals, seizing them in its sharp talons and usually swallowing them whole. It targets its prey mainly by sound, but uses its eyes to navigate between the trees in the dark. Young owls must learn these skills early in life, but for their first few months after hatching they are cared for by their parents.

Both parents **defend** their nest against predators, including bears.

TREE-STUMP NEST

Although some owls nest on the ground or even in burrows, most—including the great gray owl—nest in tree holes, old buildings, or in the abandoned nests of other birds. This great gray owl has chosen a hollow-topped tree stump, where her mottled plumage provides good camouflage. She stays close to her chicks to keep them warm while her male partner finds food for the whole family.

Day-old chicks
A female great gray owl usually lays four eggs. The chicks hatch after about four weeks, breaking out using a tough white egg tooth that these day-old chicks still have, though it will soon fall off. Their fluffy white down feathers help keep them warm on chilly nights.

First flight

At about six weeks old, young great gray owls have all their feathers. They start preparing for their first flight by stretching their wings and exercising their muscles. At first, they fly clumsily, so their father stays with them for another two or three months while they learn how to hunt for themselves.

The face feathers have not grown yet, so the young do not look like owls.

A baby owl is covered in fluffy down, helping it keep warm.

HUNGRY CHICKS

An adult great gray owl could swallow
this small mammal in one gulp,
but this female tears it into smaller
pieces to feed her chicks. Soon the
young owls will leave the nest to
roost in nearby trees, but their
mother carries on feeding them
until they are ready to fly.

TREE NURSERY

Ideal home
The colorful male wood duck and his mate must find a ready-made tree hole, because they cannot make their own. A woodpecker hole is ideal, provided the woodpeckers have left.

Just hatched
The female lays up to 15 eggs in the tree cavity and incubates them for a month until they hatch. The ducklings are covered in fluffy down, but they have only short, stumpy wings.

High and dry
Adult ducks do not bring food for their young so the ducklings need to take the plunge. Once on the ground, they start foraging for food.

WOOD DUCK

Just a day after they hatch, wood ducks take to the air—without wings!

Ducks are water birds, and many nest close to water. But the American wood duck is one of several that nest in tree holes. This gives its ducklings a problem. Like all baby ducks, they are active as soon as they hatch and need to find food, but they cannot fly. Somehow they must make their way from the nest to the water, and this often involves a dramatic leap of faith.

Just like its parents, a baby wood duck has a flattened bill adapted for sifting food from the water surface.

A wood duck's feet are equipped with sharp claws that help it perch securely in trees.

TAKING THE PLUNGE

Within a day of hatching, the ducklings are ready to go. Encouraged by their mother, who calls them from the ground below, they scramble to the entrance of the nest hole. One by one, they launch themselves into thin air—the tiny ducklings are so light that the fall doesn't hurt them.

Floating feast

Once they are on the ground, the ducklings follow their mother to the nearest water, where they can start to feed themselves right away. While she keeps watch, they gather floating seeds and snap up any insects and other small animals they can catch.

A baby duck may have to drop **60 ft** (18 m) to the ground.

Soft down feathers keep the duckling warm and help break its fall from the tree nest.

RESPONSIBLE DAD

A female African jacana defends a big territory that contains many male nesting territories. Plentiful food means she can lay a lot of eggs, so as soon as she has laid a clutch of eggs in one nest she looks for another partner, leaving the first male to take care of his eggs and young.

Floating nest
Each male jacana builds his own nest—a simple pad of leaves and waterweed. When he steps onto the nest to incubate the eggs, it is likely to sink beneath his weight, but luckily the eggs are waterproof. If a nest breaks apart, the father carries the eggs under his wings to a new location. The eggs are glossy brown with black scribble markings that help camouflage them from predators.

Under his wing
The male incubates his clutch of eggs by gathering them up under his wings. When the chicks hatch after about 25 days, they also need to be kept warm, dry, and safe from predators, so the male cares for them in the same way, tucking them under his wings. They are often so well hidden among his wing feathers that the only visible parts of them are their legs and long toes.

A jacana dad can carry **four chicks** under his wings.

Poor fliers
Young African jacanas grow proper feathers about seven weeks after hatching, but they still do not look like their parents. Even when they are fully grown, African jacanas are poor fliers, preferring to use their amazingly long-toed feet, but they can swim well.

JACANA

Baby jacanas are brought up by their fathers

Sometimes known as lily-trotters, jacanas are tropical wetland birds specialized for walking on the floating leaves of water lilies and other water plants. They have extremely long toes that spread their weight when they stand on the leaves, and this stops them sinking. Unusually, the female jacana mates with several males every breeding season, and each male raises his own family of chicks.

The chick's strong, pointed bill is ideal for seizing small prey.

Sharp-eyed chicks are alert to every hint of danger.

Young chicks are covered with soft, fluffy down feathers.

EXPLORING CHICKS

At two weeks old, chicks rely less on their father showing them what to eat, and find food for themselves. Their toes are already very long, so they can safely walk on floating plants in search of insects, worms, snails, and other small animals. The adult male keeps an eye on them, but if a chick senses danger, it can slip underwater to hide with just the bill above the surface to breathe.

WALKING ON WATER

The long toes of a jacana chick are so
effective at spreading its weight that it
can be supported by the smallest
floating leaves, almost invisible
beneath the surface. This can make it
look as if it is walking on the water itself.
But the chick may have to move fast
to avoid taking an unplanned swim!

WOODPECKER

Young woodpeckers are raised in a nest hole drilled deep into a tree by their parents

Woodpeckers are renowned for excavating holes in trees using their extra-strong bills. Many do this to find insects to eat, but during the breeding season they make much bigger cavities to nest in. Warm, dry, and safe—as long as the parents stay alert—these nesting holes make ideal nurseries for their young, and are often adopted by other birds after the woodpeckers have left.

Some woodpeckers use the same nesting hole for up to **10 years**.

ANTEATER

A woodpecker has an astonishingly long tongue, which can stick out far beyond its bill tip to gather insect prey. This green woodpecker uses it to scoop ants out of their nests, which it then takes back to feed to its chicks.

The tongue is rooted in the bird's forehead.

The sticky tongue can be pulled back into the bill.

Tongue
The woodpecker's tongue loops around its skull and out of its bill. This allows it to extend for up to a third of the bird's body length.

Perfect hideaway
When making a nesting cavity, most woodpeckers target decaying wood because it is softer and easier to work on. This female green woodpecker has found a good site and is hacking away to create an entrance hole leading to a deep nesting chamber. Here, she will raise her chicks.

FOOD DELIVERY

When woodpecker eggs hatch, the parents take turns to guard the chicks against enemies such as crows. Meanwhile, the other parent gathers insect prey. This green woodpecker and her mate may have to catch more than 1.5 million ants to feed their growing family.

The chick clings to the side of the nesting cavity so that it can be fed through the hole.

The adult woodpecker swallows prey and coughs it up to feed the chick.

GRACEFUL GLIDER

Albatrosses are specialized for flying vast distances at sea, gliding on the wind with their long, slender wings outstretched to save energy. Left to their own devices by their parents, the young learn to do this by instinct.

First flight

Four months after hatching, a young black-browed albatross finally grows all its wing feathers. But by this time, its parents are gone, so the young albatross has to make its first attempts at flight without their example to copy. It starts by stretching and flapping its wings, building up to the big moment when it launches itself into the air.

Riding the wind

Once airborne over the ocean, the young albatross gains height by gliding into the wind. It then turns and swoops down toward the waves at high speed before turning into the wind to gain height again. It can do this for hours, making use of a special adaptation that locks its wings outspread. It only needs to flap its wings when taking off from the water after seizing prey.

ALBATROSS

A young albatross soon learns to fend for itself

Like all albatrosses, the black-browed albatross lives almost exclusively at sea, soaring over the cold, stormy southern oceans that surround Antarctica. But it has to return to land to breed, nesting in crowded colonies on remote, windswept islands where there are no ground predators to threaten its young.

NESTING

Gathering in vast colonies of up to 180,000 pairs, black-browed albatrosses use mud and dried grass to build their nests. They then take turns to incubate their single egg for 10 weeks. The chick has a coat of downy feathers when it hatches, but its parents still need to keep it warm in the chilly climate. After 20 days it is big enough to be left alone while both parents hunt at sea.

Food delivery
During the first days of their chick's life the parents take turns to gather prey at sea, hunting for fish, squid, and shrimplike krill. They return to land with bellyfuls of half-digested food and energy-rich stomach oil, some of which they cough up to feed the chick in its nest. The unfledged chicks grow so well on the fat-rich food that they become heavier than their parents.

The dark line over the adult's eyes gives the black-browed albatross its name.

An adult albatross can live up to 70 years.

The chick has a sharp, hooked bill—ideal for seizing slippery fish and squid.

The young chick's soft, fluffy white down helps keep out the cold.

LONG WAIT

Sitting patiently on its mud nest, this black-browed albatross chick hopes one of its parents will soon return with food. It may have to wait for several days while the parents fly far over the ocean in search of prey, but the chick's rich, oily diet keeps it going until its next meal.

GOLDEN EAGLE

Eagle chicks fight to survive their first few days

The golden eagle is one of the most powerful and widespread birds of prey, found in wild landscapes worldwide, north of the equator. It hunts by soaring on rising air currents while watching for prey on the ground, and diving to seize it in its huge, sharp talons. Adult eagles pair for life, occupying a big territory with several nest sites, and choose a different one to use each year.

If food is short the bigger chick may bully the smaller one to stop it taking its share.

HEIR AND A SPARE

The female lays two or three eggs. She starts incubating the first egg right away, so it hatches first. By the time the last egg hatches, the oldest chick is big enough to seize most of the food brought to the nest. If prey is scarce, this ensures the survival of at least one chick. The youngest chick will only make it if food is abundant, or if the older one dies.

Even at this age, the chick has a hooked bill for dealing with prey.

Mealtime

Prey brought to the nest by the male is torn into small pieces by the female using her hooked bill. She then feeds some of these pieces to the young. When a chick is about a month old it starts copying her, tearing its own mouthfuls from the prey.

It takes a baby eagle **36 hours** to chip its way out of its egg.

CLIFF NEST

Some golden eagles nest in tall trees, but they prefer sheer cliffs with remote ledges that are only accessible from the air. Here the pair build a big nest of sticks, repairing and enlarging it each season before laying any eggs.

A newly hatched chick spends most of its time lying down in the nest.

Hatching

The eggs are incubated for about 43 days, mainly by the female while the male keeps her supplied with food. The chicks hatch covered with fluffy white down, but their parents must keep them warm for at least 20 days. The first to hatch soon starts feeding on prey brought by the male, almost doubling in size by the time the next egg starts hatching.

Ready to fly

It is unusual for more than one golden eagle chick to survive the first three weeks of life. But for these long-lived birds, raising one chick each season is enough. By the time the chick is four weeks old, dark body feathers have largely replaced its white down, and within another seven weeks the young eagle will be ready to make its first flight.

REPTILES

Most female reptiles lay eggs. They hide them somewhere safe and warm, but then usually forget them. When the babies finally hatch, they have to fend for themselves, relying on instinct to find their own food and hide from danger. If it is not very careful, this young Komodo dragon may even be eaten by one of its own parents.

BREAKING OUT

After developing in the egg for about seven weeks, a baby green sea turtle is ready to hatch. Cutting its way out of its leathery egg, the baby turtle enjoys its first breath of fresh air before facing the most dangerous phase of its life—its journey to the sea.

A small, toothlike projection from the baby's beak helps it cut its way out of the egg.

Sea turtle eggs have flexible shells, unlike the hard, brittle eggs of birds.

LIFE CYCLE

Hidden nest
A female green sea turtle returns to the beach where she hatched to lay her eggs. Some swim more than 1,600 miles (2,600 km) to get there. She digs a hole in the sand and lays up to 200 eggs, then covers them up and goes back out to sea.

Hatching out
A newly hatched baby turtle usually stays hidden under the sand for a few days until all its siblings have hatched, too. Then one night they all dig their way out of the sand at once, because this is much safer than braving the long journey to the sea alone.

SEA TURTLE

A baby turtle is lucky to survive its first few days

Although sea turtles are beautifully adapted for life in the water, they cannot breed in the open ocean. Each female must come ashore to lay her eggs in warm sand above the tide line. She slips back out to sea, leaving her babies to hatch and make their own hazardous way across the beach to the relative safety of the waves.

The baby's flippers are fully formed when it hatches, helping it swim when it reaches the sea.

INSIDE THE EGG

Inside its soft shell, a turtle's egg is similar to a bird's egg. The developing embryo draws all the nutrients it needs from the yolk, and any waste is stored in the allantois until the baby breaks out of the egg.

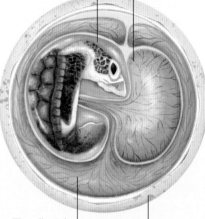

A fluid-filled sac called the amnion protects the embryo.

The yolk sac supplies the embryo with food.

The allantois removes waste.

Shell

Desperate race
As the baby turtles scamper across the sand toward the breaking waves, they make easy targets for an army of predators, including gulls, foxes, and even hungry ghost crabs. Many do not survive the trip, and there are more dangers in the sea.

Life at sea
If they reach the water and manage to avoid the hunters lurking offshore, baby green sea turtles head out to sea. They roam the oceans for up to five years before settling in warm, shallow, coastal seas, where they feed mainly on seaweeds and seagrasses.

On guard

The crocodile mother digs a hole along a sandy river bank and lays up to 80 eggs. She then covers the nest with sand. Both parents take turns guarding the nest for about three months. When the crocodile mother hears the hatchling calls, she unearths the nest. The baby crocodiles then start to crack the shells, using a tiny egg tooth—a hardened piece of skin on a hatchling's upper jaw. Their mom also helps them break free by gently cracking the shells with her teeth.

The nostrils, like the eyes and ears, are on the top of the head so it can hide just below the surface of the water and still keep breathing.

MALE OR FEMALE?

A hatchling's sex is determined by the temperature of the nest during development. If the temperature is warm, males are produced. But if the temperature of the nest is either very low or very high, females develop.

The eyes are similar to a cat's eyes—in bright sunlight, the pupils close to vertical slits but at nighttime they open wide to increase sensitivity.

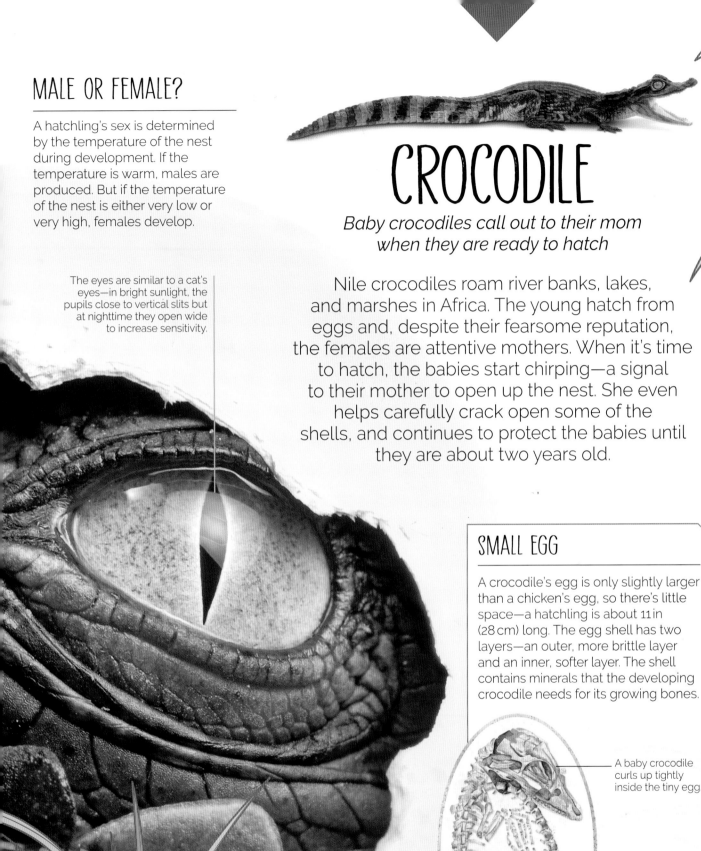

CROCODILE

Baby crocodiles call out to their mom when they are ready to hatch

Nile crocodiles roam river banks, lakes, and marshes in Africa. The young hatch from eggs and, despite their fearsome reputation, the females are attentive mothers. When it's time to hatch, the babies start chirping—a signal to their mother to open up the nest. She even helps carefully crack open some of the shells, and continues to protect the babies until they are about two years old.

SMALL EGG

A crocodile's egg is only slightly larger than a chicken's egg, so there's little space—a hatchling is about 11 in (28 cm) long. The egg shell has two layers—an outer, more brittle layer and an inner, softer layer. The shell contains minerals that the developing crocodile needs for its growing bones.

A baby crocodile curls up tightly inside the tiny egg.

The outer layer is similar to a bird's egg.

Although Nile crocodiles might reach over 16 ft (5 m) in length, hatchlings are only about 11 in (28 cm) long, so they are easy targets for predators such as lizards and snakes. The mother protects her newborn by carrying them in her mouth to the water's edge, where they feed on insects and fish.

SHORT-TERM CARE

Like most other kinds of gecko, a female leaf-tailed gecko may lay up to three clutches of two or three eggs each year. She starts at the beginning of the tropical rainy season, when the wet weather ensures that the eggs are unlikely to dry out.

Spherical eggs

Most reptiles lay leathery eggs, but the perfectly round eggs of the leaf-tailed gecko become hard-shelled soon after hatching, more like the eggs of birds. The female deposits them among the moist foliage of living or dead plants, or in the layer of dead leaves lying on the forest floor. After laying her eggs she goes away, trusting the tropical climate to keep them warm enough to develop.

Hatching out

The eggs can take up to four months to hatch—a surprisingly long time for such a small animal. The young leaf-tailed geckos emerge as miniature versions of their parents, and are able to climb and hunt small insects within a short time of hatching. If they manage to avoid being picked off by predators, they may live for up to five years.

New look
Like other lizards, a gecko regularly sheds its scratched and stained outer skin. It does this most often when it is young and growing fast. The skin peels away in large pieces, revealing a fresh new layer beneath.

PERFECT CAMOUFLAGE

Only the baby gecko's eyes gives away the fact that this is a live animal and not a dead leaf. This baby is actually clinging to the head of its mother, whose camouflage is even more effective. As long as they both avoid moving, they will be safe from any animals that hunt by sight in the forests of their native Madagascar.

LEAF-TAILED GECKO

A baby leaf-tailed gecko can be hard to spot

Geckos are mainly tropical lizards that typically have amazing climbing skills, thanks to their adhesive toes. They mostly hunt insects at night, lying low by day and relying on their camouflage to conceal them from predators. From the moment it hatches, a leaf-tailed gecko's camouflage is so good that it can hide in plain sight.

Each toe has a pad that clings to flat surfaces like a magnet.

HATCHLINGS

A mother Komodo dragon takes full responsibility for caring for her eggs—her mate performs no fatherly duties. She can even—on occasion—lay eggs that produce babies without mating with a male. This might be useful if she cannot find a mate, but these unfertilized eggs only hatch into males.

Clutch of eggs
About 20 eggs are laid in a hollow or in the abandoned, twig-lined nest of a particular bird, a scrub fowl. The female Komodo dragon protects these for about eight months, warning off other Komodo dragons who would eat them.

Ready to hatch
The baby Komodo dragons use a hardened bit of skin on their snout—an egg tooth—to break free of the eggshell. It's an exhausting process for them and, once free, they are on their own and vulnerable to predators.

Baby Komodo dragons are colorfully patterned—adults are gray.

KOMODO DRAGON

After hatching, a baby Komodo dragon heads straight for a tree

A newborn Komodo is under threat right after breaking free of its egg—if it doesn't escape up a tree very quickly, its own parents will eat it. On hatching, these lizards are only about 16 in (40 cm) in length, but they grow to be the largest of all lizards, reaching lengths around 10 ft (3 m). They become formidable hunters, ambushing prey using sharp claws and savage bites.

Komodo dragons are found only on a few **Indonesian islands**.

LIFE IN THE TREES

To stay alive, a young Komodo dragon must stick to the safety of trees until it is about two years old—when it's big enough to come down from the tree and not feel vulnerable. In these first years, it feeds on snakes, birds, insects, and small lizards. It must size up other young Komodo dragons and decide whether to eat them or run away.

Young lizards don't have the same tough scales as their parents—they develop these when they are older.

Like their parents, baby Komodo dragons have excellent daytime vision for spotting prey.

CHAMELEON

A chameleon is born with the hunting instinct

Best known for their ability to change color depending on their mood, chameleons are specialized insect hunters that mainly live in the trees of tropical forests. Like other lizards, they mostly lay eggs. But some, including Jackson's chameleon, retain the eggs in their bodies until they hatch, so they give birth to live young that are like baby versions of the adults.

A female Jackson's chameleon has up to **30 babies**.

MINIATURE ADULT

When it grows up, a male Jackson's chameleon has three long horns for sparring with rival males. Apart from this and its small size, a newborn baby looks almost identical. It has the same adaptations for stalking and seizing insect prey, which it knows how to do without being taught.

ON TARGET

A young chameleon starts hunting insects soon after it is born. Targeting prey with its highly mobile eyes, the chameleon creeps up on it very slowly, then suddenly seizes the prey with a split-second flick of its incredibly long, sticky-tipped tongue. Reeling its prize back into its mouth, the young chameleon gulps it down and looks for another victim.

Only the male Jackson's chameleon has these long horns.

Peeling skin
A Jackson's chameleon is just 2 in (5.5 cm) long when it is born. As it grows, a young chameleon sheds its scaly skin at intervals, peeling it off in big flakes over a period of about 15 minutes.

A chameleon's eyes can swivel to look in two directions at once, or focus on the same target.

Special light-reflecting crystals in the chameleon's skin change position to make the lizard change color. This young chameleon has turned brown for camouflage.

Easy targets

Tadpoles and frogs are preyed upon by a wide variety of predators, including grass snakes and birds such as this kingfisher. They are easy targets as they are unable to defend themselves and, as tadpoles, are particularly visible in a pond.

A transparent inner eyelid helps protect the eye when underwater and keeps it moist when on land.

Tiny teeth in the upper jaw are used to grip prey.

EARLY LIFE IN WATER

Left to take care of itself, the bean-size tadpole stays in the water where it was spawned. It grazes on algae, but later eats tiny animal prey. This helps provide nutrients needed to grow legs and complete its metamorphosis.

SHAPE-SHIFTERS

The European common frog undergoes a series of amazing changes to become an adult. The process takes about 16 weeks.

Egg
Each jellylike capsule contains a tiny black egg. It takes a few days for the embryo to develop into a legless tadpole.

A tough jelly coating protects the egg.

Tadpole
After about two weeks, the tadpole breaks through the jelly. It has gills for absorbing oxygen from the water and a tail fin that wriggles from side to side to propel the tadpole through the water.

The tail shrivels to a stump.

Froglet
By 14 weeks, the tadpole has turned into a tiny froglet. It has both back and front legs, and its swimming tail has shrunk—the tail is absorbed into the body, providing nutrients for the growing froglet. It is ready to climb out of the water.

Adult frog
The frog hunts small animals on land, but can still swim well in water.

An adult frog is about 4 in (10 cm) long.

FROG SPAWN

In early spring European common frogs return to water to breed. The female lays up to 2,000 eggs in clumps called frog spawn. She then abandons the eggs. Many are eaten by predators, but laying so many means that some will survive into adulthood.

FROM EGG TO LARVA

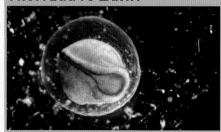

Egg
A female lays about 100-200 eggs at a time. The dark brown eggs are laid in a transparent jelly.

Embryo
Still protected by a layer of jelly, the embryo now has a noticeable backbone. It is tiny, at a length of just ¼ in (5 mm).

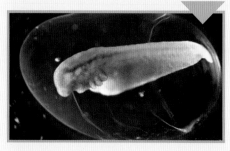

Larva
A body fin is now developing along the back, which will help the larva move in its water home. The tail has begun to grow.

Hatched larva
The larva feeds on tiny animals, such as water fleas, which provide the protein needed to develop legs.

AXOLOTL

An axolotl is a salamander that never fully grows up

Most amphibians, such as frogs and salamanders, start off their lives as swimming larvae, or tadpoles, with gills for breathing underwater. Then they change their gills for lungs as they develop into air-breathing adults. But a Mexican salamander called the axolotl keeps its gills throughout its life and stays in the water. It develops lungs, too—but they stay small and are only useful for taking the occasional gulp of air.

Axolotls **burrow under the sand** to escape from predators.

STAYING UNDERWATER

A young axolotl grows legs just like ordinary frogs and salamanders but doesn't use them for walking around on land. Instead, it clambers around on the bottom of a pond or lake among thick pondweed, where it hunts for worms and other small prey. Its feathery gills absorb oxygen from the surrounding water, helping it breathe submerged just like a fish.

A NEW LIMB

Most animals—just like humans—cannot regrow lost body parts, but salamanders, including axolotls, can do just this. If they lose a limb in an accident, they regenerate a new one. They can even rebuild damaged vital organs, such as their heart, brain, or eyes.

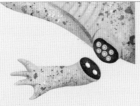

Limb lost
A leg may be lost due to another axolotl biting one off while protecting its territory—axolotls tend to live alone and like their own space.

Regrowth
The leg begins to bud soon after the limb is lost, and the bones begin to grow. It can take two to three months to grow a complete leg.

New limb
The replacement limb is a perfect duplicate of the one that was lost. If this particular limb is lost again, the same process will be repeated.

The adult has a long dorsal fin that runs along its back, a juvenile feature that other salamanders lose.

The feathery gills are filled with blood to absorb oxygen.

An axolotl can take in air through its mouth to breathe if necessary.

METAMORPHOSIS

Although most eastern newts have three life stages—larva, eft, and adult—their development varies a lot from place to place. In some parts of North America, there is no eft stage and larvae transform straight into adults. This happens in open, sandy habitats, where there is no good ground cover for the efts.

Larvae

The larvae hatch from fertilized eggs that are stuck to pondweed or dead leaves. They swim by beating a finlike tail and breathe with feathery gills, before growing limbs in preparation for their later life on land. A diet of tiny aquatic animals, such as water fleas, supplies the nourishment they need to develop.

Adults

After two to five months, most larvae develop into air-breathing newts with lungs instead of gills, and become breeding adults with a brown back and yellow belly. But in some locations, adults keep their gills and stay underwater, and only later develop lungs if their pond dries up.

Vulnerable time
Adult newts lose their juvenile red color, turning brown and yellow—and with it they lose much of their protective poison, too. For safety, they rely instead on the cover of thick weed in the ponds where they breed. But a sharp-eyed heron shows that hiding away doesn't always work.

The skin on the back of the baby, where it is more likely to be attacked, is more poisonous than the skin on its belly.

TOXIC BABY

A tiny baby eastern newt searching the mossy ground for insect prey might be easy pickings for a reptile or bird. But its poison makes it taste disgusting. This powerful defense mechanism keeps away predators, such as garter snakes and hawks that remember trying to eat one. The youngest and smallest efts are the most toxic—they can be 10 times more poisonous than adult newts.

NEWT

A baby amphibian that is protected by poison

Newts are lizard-shaped amphibians with lives that are split between water and land. They change from swimming larvae into walking juveniles called efts, before growing into adults that return to the water to breed and complete their life cycle. Most defenseless newts are nocturnal, but efts of the eastern newt from North America can risk being active by day—their red coloring is a warning to predators that their skin is poisonous.

The coarse skin is bright red or orange, and often has lines of spots.

FISH

A typical baby fish needs a lot of luck to survive. Most fish scatter thousands of eggs in the water, where they are swept away by currents and often devoured by other animals. The babies that hatch from the eggs are just as vulnerable. But a few fish take more care of their young. This male yellowhead jawfish even keeps all its eggs safe in its mouth until they are ready to hatch.

HATCHING TIME

Eggs

A clutch of up to 1,000 eggs are laid, each no bigger than ⅛ in (4 mm). After about a week, they begin to hatch but only at nighttime.

Larva

After hatching, the larva spends up to 12 days in the open ocean, drifting in the current before it returns to the reef as juvenile clown fish.

Juvenile

As the clown fish grows, it becomes more colorful and its distinctive stripes emerge—one around its head and another further down it's body.

Adult

Common clown fish reach a length of about 4 in (11 cm). As an adult, it now settles down to life in the protection of a sea anemone.

The male keeps a beady eye on the eggs, picking out and eating any that are damaged or dead.

Males first

The eggs are laid on a rock that has been pre-cleaned by the male, with a sticky thread attaching each egg to the rock. A mass of silvery eyes is very noticeable after the fifth day. All will grow up to become males first, before changing their sex to replace breeding females that die. These eggs are close to hatching, and once hatched, parental care will stop.

CLOWN FISH

As eggs, clown fish are carefully guarded, but upon hatching, they are on their own

The common clown fish lives in the warm, tropical waters of coral reefs. Eggs are laid on a rock near a sea anemone's stinging tentacles and then watched over by the parents. The anemone provides protection for both the eggs and their parents. On hatching, the larvae are transparent and without stripes—their colors develop as they grow.

A SAFE NURSERY

Once the eggs are laid, the male spends much of his time taking care of them. He uses his fins to fan them, which helps keep the eggs supplied with oxygen. Meanwhile, the female takes on sentry duty, watching over both the male and the eggs and chasing off potential predators.

SEAHORSE

Baby seahorses have an unusual start in life

Seahorses live in shallow tropical and temperate waters throughout the world. They are unusual-looking fish with their horselike heads and upright swimming action. But the most extraordinary feature of all is the fact that the male seahorses give birth to their babies instead of the females. Once the baby seahorses are released into the ocean, they must fend for themselves. If they survive the perils of ocean life, they can live up to five years. But most of these rice-size young won't make it to adulthood.

MAKING A SEAHORSE

The eggs develop very quickly inside the pouch, which expands to accommodate the growing embryos. Several weeks later, when the babies are fully developed, the seahorse dad's body contracts, pushing out the tiny seahorses.

Embryo develops	Eye lenses form	Yolk sac gets smaller	Baby seahorse emerges
1–3 days	7–10 days	14–17 days	24 days

Finding a mate
Female seahorses often compete with each other to win the chance to mate with the male (shown here on the left). To attract the male, they show off their bony ridges and brighten up by changing their skin color.

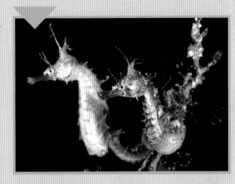

Dancing seahorses
When the male seahorse has chosen his partner, they meet up again in the morning. They perform a synchronized swim-dance that can last for hours or even days.

Transferring the eggs
After the dance, the seahorse mother transfers her eggs into the male's brood pouch—a pocket on the male's belly. She uses her egg-laying tube called an ovipositor to safely place the unfertilized eggs into his pouch.

JAWFISH

The male jawfish keeps his unhatched babies safe in his mouth

Most sea fish lay vast quantities of eggs—these drift with the ocean currents, and most of them get eaten by other fish. The jawfish gets around this problem by protecting its eggs in a surprising way. The male gathers them all into his mouth, and keeps them there until they hatch. But once hatched, each tiny jawfish is on its own.

A male jawfish can hold up to **1,500 eggs** in his mouth.

PRECIOUS MOUTHFUL

When the female jawfish lays her eggs, the male fertilizes them before scooping them up into his mouth and keeping them there for a week or more. Occasionally, he spits the eggs out and gathers them up again to give them a wash and make sure they get enough oxygen.

MAKING A HOME

Yellow-headed jawfish live on or near coral reefs in the Caribbean region. When each young fish finally settles on the seabed, it digs a burrow downward into the sand and lines it with stones to stop it collapsing. The jawfish keeps its home in good shape, using its mouth to add or remove sand.

SHIFTING SAND

SITTING TIGHT

With his mouth full of eggs and unable to eat, the male jawfish spends nearly all his time in his burrow.

New life

After seven to nine days, the jawfish eggs hatch. The tiny, transparent baby fish swim out of their father's mouth and up into open water. They spend some time drifting in plankton before growing into burrowing adults.

The baby jawfish are visible growing inside the soft-coated eggs, which clump together in a sticky ball while inside dad's mouth.

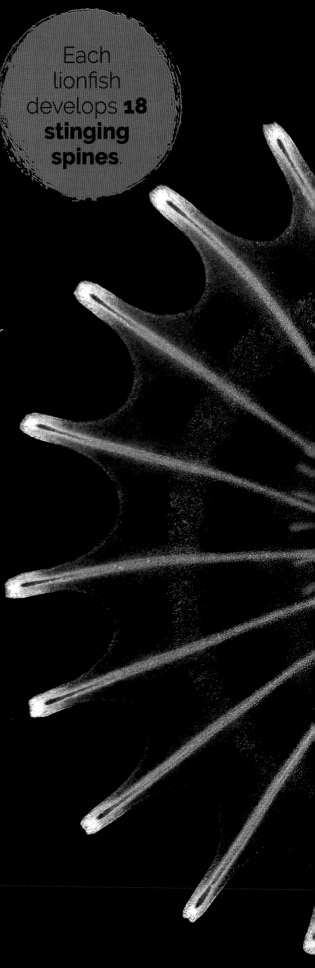

LIONFISH

An ocean fish defended by spines

Like many ocean fish, the lionfish scatters thousands of eggs that hatch into tiny babies. Each baby grows spiny fins that fan outward in the water and make them a difficult mouthful for bigger predators. But as they get bigger, they develop more impressive protection—some of their spines turn venomous and can inflict an agonizing sting.

Each lionfish develops **18 stinging spines**.

Lurking lionfish
Down on the seabed, lionfish become formidable predators—by spreading their spiny fins, they scare fish and crabs so they get cornered against the rocks and coral. Then they use their big mouths to swallow their prey in a single gulp. Lionfish have few enemies—this has enabled them to invade new habitats around the world.

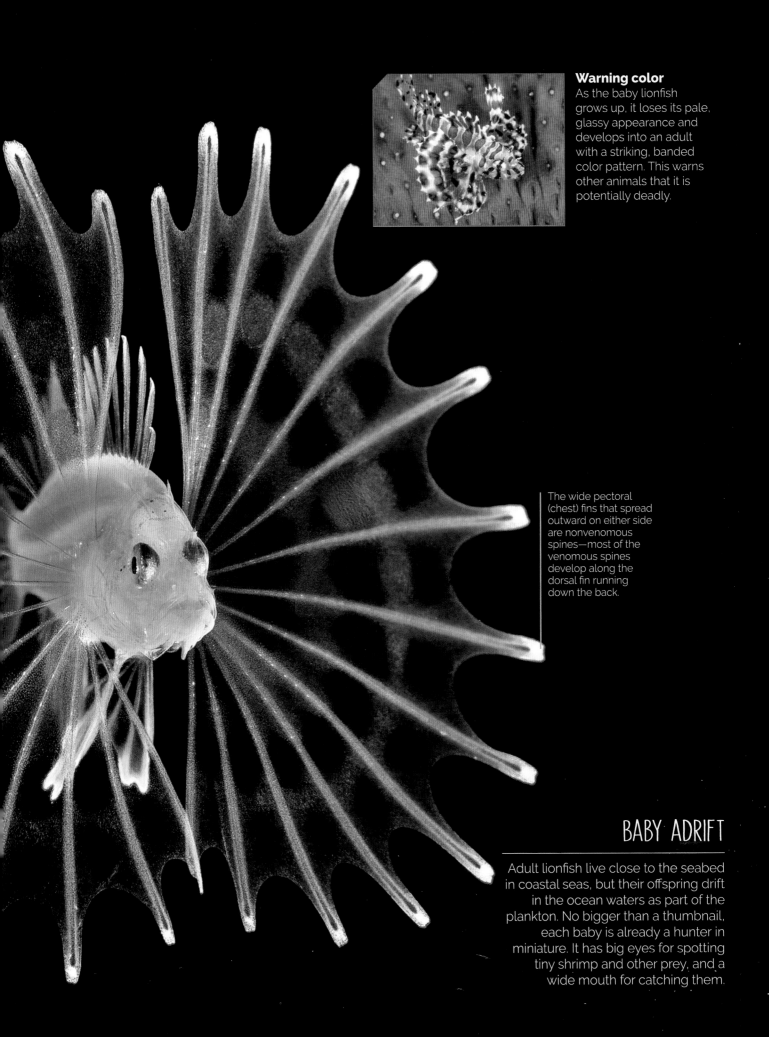

Warning color
As the baby lionfish grows up, it loses its pale, glassy appearance and develops into an adult with a striking, banded color pattern. This warns other animals that it is potentially deadly.

The wide pectoral (chest) fins that spread outward on either side are nonvenomous spines—most of the venomous spines develop along the dorsal fin running down the back.

BABY ADRIFT

Adult lionfish live close to the seabed in coastal seas, but their offspring drift in the ocean waters as part of the plankton. No bigger than a thumbnail, each baby is already a hunter in miniature. It has big eyes for spotting tiny shrimp and other prey, and a wide mouth for catching them.

INVERTEBRATES

Most of the animals on Earth are invertebrates.
They range from tiny, scurrying mites to giant squid,
and include worms, snails, insects, spiders, crabs,
jellyfish, and flowerlike corals. They nearly all lay
eggs, but while some hatch as miniatures of their
parents, others begin life in a quite different
form. This swallowtail butterfly was once a
wingless caterpillar, but look at it now!

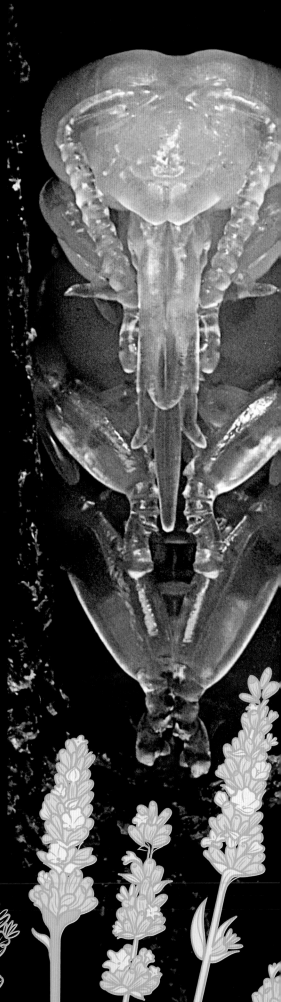

HONEYBEE

Honeybees raise their young in cells made out of wax

Honeybees live in huge families ruled over by a single breeding female, the queen. She lays all the eggs—up to 2,500 per day—in the cells of a wax honeycomb created by thousands of worker bees, which are all her daughters. The workers defend the nest with their stings and gather sweet nectar from flowers, turning it into honey to feed the queen and her young.

LIFE CYCLE

The queen lays one egg in each cell of the honeycomb. After three days, each egg hatches as a legless larva, which is normally fed a mixture of honey and flower pollen by the workers. When it is fully grown, it is sealed into its cell and changes into a pupa—the stage when it is transformed into an adult. About 21 days after the egg was laid, a new bee pushes out of the cell and joins the workforce.

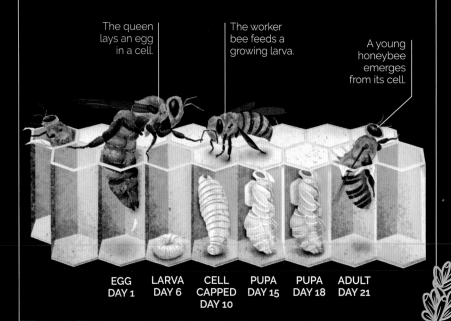

The queen lays an egg in a cell.

The worker bee feeds a growing larva.

A young honeybee emerges from its cell.

| EGG DAY 1 | LARVA DAY 6 | CELL CAPPED DAY 10 | PUPA DAY 15 | PUPA DAY 18 | ADULT DAY 21 |

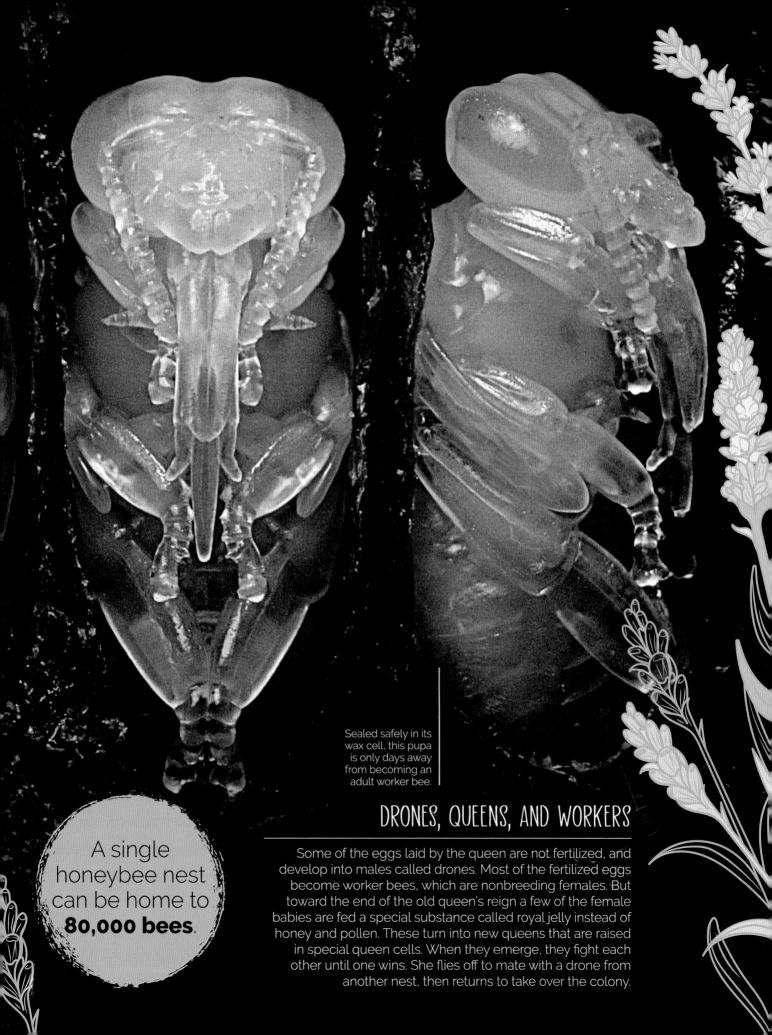

Sealed safely in its wax cell, this pupa is only days away from becoming an adult worker bee.

A single honeybee nest can be home to **80,000 bees**.

DRONES, QUEENS, AND WORKERS

Some of the eggs laid by the queen are not fertilized, and develop into males called drones. Most of the fertilized eggs become worker bees, which are nonbreeding females. But toward the end of the old queen's reign a few of the female babies are fed a special substance called royal jelly instead of honey and pollen. These turn into new queens that are raised in special queen cells. When they emerge, they fight each other until one wins. She flies off to mate with a drone from another nest, then returns to take over the colony.

BUSY BEES

A honeycomb is made up of thousands of tubular cells. Some are used for storing honey, but many of the open cells seen here hold a legless larva, which is fed by the busy worker bees. Each capped cell contains a developing bee pupa—the stage where its eyes, wings, and legs develop before it emerges as an adult.

PARENT BUG

The babies of this species of shield bug enjoy the devoted care of their mother

Most insects lay their eggs and then abandon them. Many of the eggs do not survive to hatch, and even if they do, the babies are easy prey for other animals. But a female parent bug tries to prevent this by protecting her eggs and young, shielding them from attack until they can take care of themselves.

STAGE BY STAGE

Many insects are described as bugs, but a true bug is a special type of insect that eats liquid food, sucking it up through a sharp-tipped tube. Parent bugs drink the sugary sap of plants. They hatch as tiny six-legged nymphs and develop through five stages, shedding their skins at the end of each stage to emerge in a slightly different form. Each stage is called an instar.

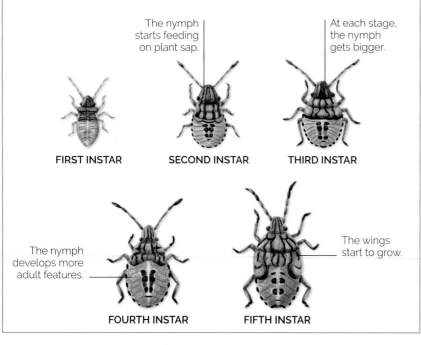

The nymph starts feeding on plant sap.

At each stage, the nymph gets bigger.

FIRST INSTAR

SECOND INSTAR

THIRD INSTAR

The nymph develops more adult features.

The wings start to grow.

FOURTH INSTAR

FIFTH INSTAR

CLOSE GUARD

A female parent bug guards her newly hatched babies by crouching over them. If any slip away, she guides them back to safety. The tiny nymphs do not need to feed on sap at this stage, but as they grow their mother leads them to parts of the plant where sap is easy to drink.

The adult bug has a pair of wings folded over her tail end.

The parent bug's **childcare** has been known about since 1764.

Egg cluster
Each female parent bug attaches 40 to 50 eggs to the underside of a birch leaf. She arranges them in a roughly diamond-shaped cluster that matches her own shape. This allows her to conceal the clutch of eggs from hungry birds and other enemies by covering them with her body.

The parent bug belongs to a family of insects called shield bugs—named for the shield-like shape of their bodies.

Chemical defense
When the mother bug senses danger, she leans toward the threat to shield her family with her body. She may fan her wings with a loud buzz, and if this doesn't work she can drive an enemy away by releasing a foul-smelling chemical spray.

All the tiny nymphs stay clustered within the span of their mother's legs.

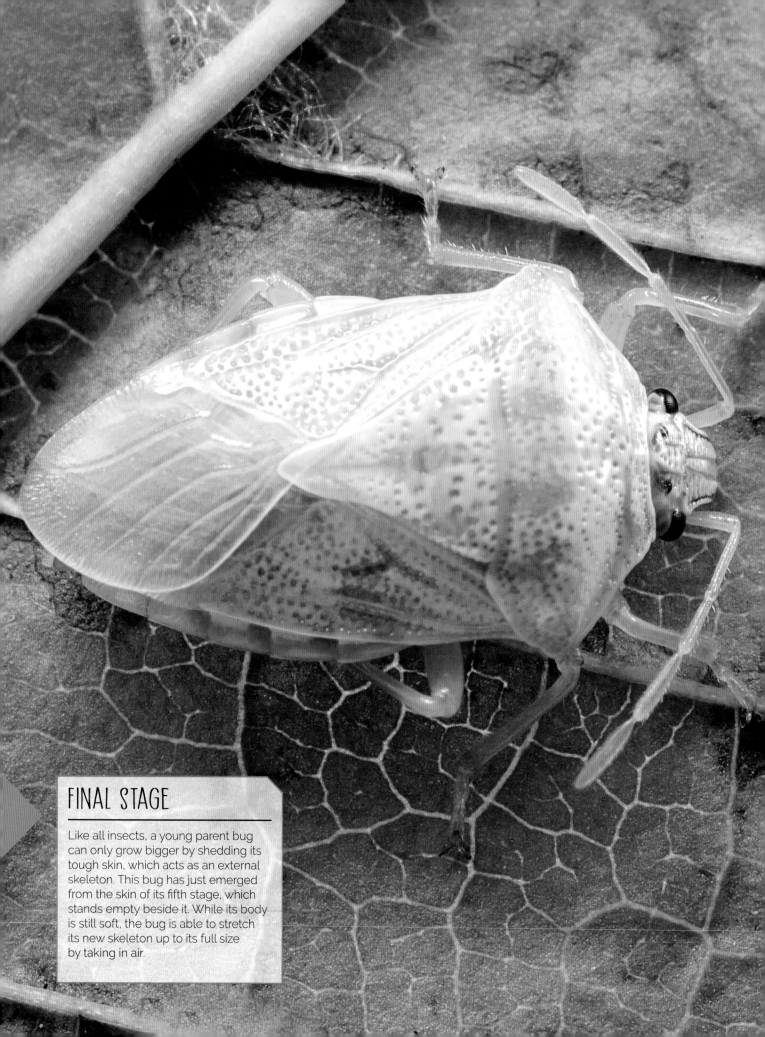

FINAL STAGE

Like all insects, a young parent bug can only grow bigger by shedding its tough skin, which acts as an external skeleton. This bug has just emerged from the skin of its fifth stage, which stands empty beside it. While its body is still soft, the bug is able to stretch its new skeleton up to its full size by taking in air.

DRIFTING IN THE OCEAN

Since mantis shrimp rarely stray far from their burrows, they need a way of making sure their babies find somewhere else to live. Luckily, their young are so light that they can drift away with the ocean currents.

Motherly care

A female peacock mantis shrimp carries her eggs in her front limbs to protect them from fish and other hungry animals. This makes sure that most of the eggs survive until they are ready to hatch. But after that, the young mantis shrimp are on their own.

Newborn

Each mantis shrimp egg hatches into a tiny, spiky larva that swims among the plankton in open water. Here, it then develops into a bigger clawed larva with stalked eyes, before going through a final change, where it turns into an adult and settles on the seabed.

MANTIS SHRIMP

A baby mantis shrimp is a homeless hunter

Mantis shrimp are fearsomely efficient ambush hunters that lurk in burrows on the beds of tropical shallow seas, often on coral reefs. But their young drift among the plankton of the open ocean, preying on any other small animals that have the bad luck to run into them.

Barbed claws open up to grab unsuspecting victims.

Specialized 3D vision ensures that the shrimp always hits its target.

The club-like claws are folded away.

Packing a punch

Some types of adult mantis shrimp have sharp claws, and use them to stab soft-bodied prey. Others have heavier claws, which they use to smash the hard shells of crabs and snails. Their drifting larvae are almost as deadly to small floating animals.

Like adults, mantis shrimp larvae have compound eyes that are set on stalks. The eyes can move independently of one another, helping them spot prey and danger.

Mantis shrimp have forked antennae for sensing their surroundings.

GHOSTLY PREDATOR

Other creatures drifting among the plankton may not notice a transparent mantis shrimp larva nearby. But it can certainly see them, and within seconds it will seize them in its powerful claws.

The transparent body helps the larva stay invisible in open water.

A female mantis shrimp may carry up to **50,000 eggs**.

BUTTERFLY

An insect that starts life as a caterpillar turns into a winged butterfly

A butterfly spends most of its life as a hungry caterpillar, munching through leaves and growing bigger every day. It puts on so much weight that it has to shed its skin several times as it grows. When it sheds its last caterpillar skin it emerges as a chrysalis—a non-feeding stage when its body is transformed into that of a dazzling adult butterfly.

Looking like a snake's tongue, the defensive organ smells of rotting pineapple.

Smelly defense
Caterpillars are eaten by many other animals, including baby birds fed by their parents. Many are well camouflaged, but this swallowtail caterpillar tries to scare enemies away by flicking a forked, strong-smelling organ in their faces.

The skin of the chrysalis is left behind as the butterfly begins its adult life.

ALL CHANGE

Egg
A female swallowtail butterfly lays hundreds of tiny eggs on the leaves of a marsh plant called milk parsley. At first, each egg is pale yellow, but it darkens as the caterpillar develops inside. After about ten days it hatches, and starts nibbling at the leaves.

Caterpillar
The young swallowtail caterpillar is camouflaged so it looks like a bird dropping. But when it sheds its skin for the third time it emerges with bright, red-dotted, green and black stripes. This pattern may warn hungry birds that it tastes bad.

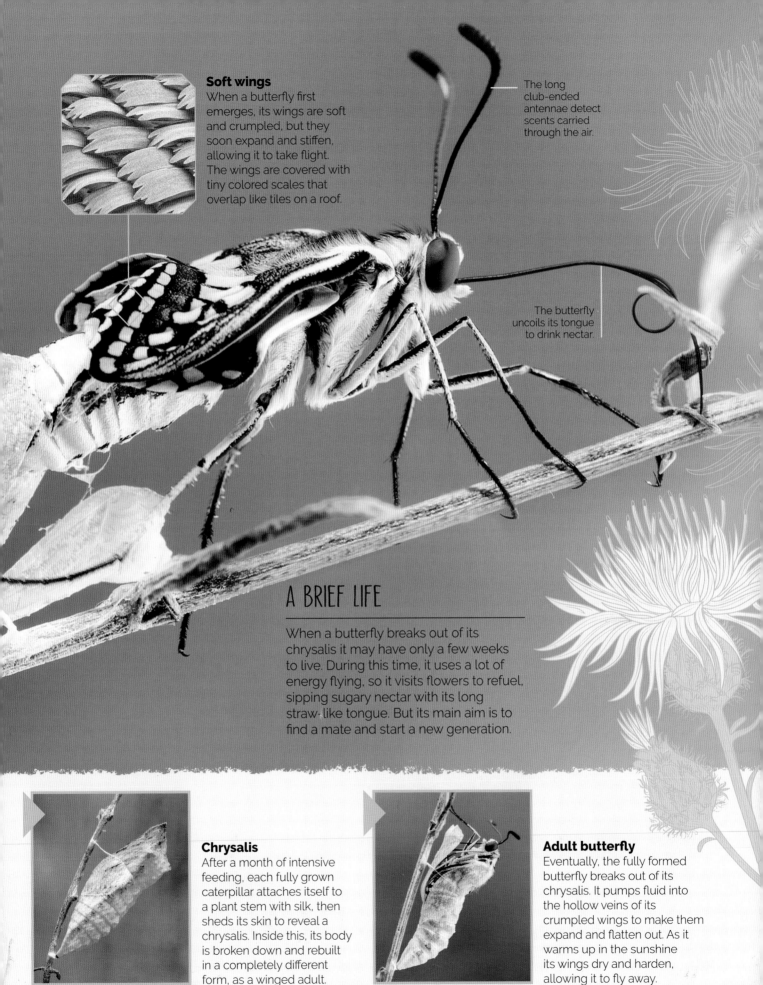

Soft wings
When a butterfly first emerges, its wings are soft and crumpled, but they soon expand and stiffen, allowing it to take flight. The wings are covered with tiny colored scales that overlap like tiles on a roof.

The long club-ended antennae detect scents carried through the air.

The butterfly uncoils its tongue to drink nectar.

A BRIEF LIFE

When a butterfly breaks out of its chrysalis it may have only a few weeks to live. During this time, it uses a lot of energy flying, so it visits flowers to refuel, sipping sugary nectar with its long straw-like tongue. But its main aim is to find a mate and start a new generation.

Chrysalis
After a month of intensive feeding, each fully grown caterpillar attaches itself to a plant stem with silk, then sheds its skin to reveal a chrysalis. Inside this, its body is broken down and rebuilt in a completely different form, as a winged adult.

Adult butterfly
Eventually, the fully formed butterfly breaks out of its chrysalis. It pumps fluid into the hollow veins of its crumpled wings to make them expand and flatten out. As it warms up in the sunshine its wings dry and harden, allowing it to fly away.

WOLF SPIDER

When baby wolf spiders hatch, they climb onto their mother's back

Found all over the world in almost every kind of habitat, wolf spiders get their name from the way they chase their prey like tiny wolves instead of trapping it in webs. There are more than 2,400 species, and in those studied the mothers take great care of their young, typically carrying them on their back until they are big enough to live on their own.

Wolf spiders are the **only spiders** known to carry their babies on their backs.

FREE RIDE

After the baby spiders have hatched, the wolf spider mother discards the empty egg sac and the spiderlings climb up onto her abdomen. She then carries them on her back for a week or so until they are ready to make their own way in the world. During this time, the mother keeps her babies away from predators and other danger.

The egg sac is made of a mat of special silk that looks like paper.

A safe start
A female wolf spider places her eggs inside a hollow ball of silk and attaches the sac to the silk-spinning spinnerets at the back end of her body—so she carries it wherever she goes. In other species she keeps the sac in a burrow. The eggs of this burrowing wolf spider are ready to hatch, and she cuts the sac open with her fangs so the babies can emerge.

Spiderlings

While the babies are on their mother's back, they do not eat. But soon hunger or the instinct to hunt makes them leave. Each one spins a strand of silk that catches the wind, lifting them upward and away to land elsewhere.

A wolf spider may carry 50 to 100 spiderlings. If any fall off, she waits for them to climb back on.

Baby spiders on their mother's back link legs to help them cling on.

OCTOPUS

A baby octopus must learn to take care of itself as soon as it hatches from its egg

An octopus is an astonishing creature. It is a marine mollusk—a relative of snails and clams—yet it is very intelligent, has an excellent memory, and can use tools. Since it has no bones, it can squeeze its rubbery, eight-armed body through the narrowest gaps, and can even escape danger by jet propulsion. After mating, a female southern keeled octopus lays clusters of eggs that hatch as miniature octopuses. These live like their parents, seizing and eating tiny crabs and similar animals.

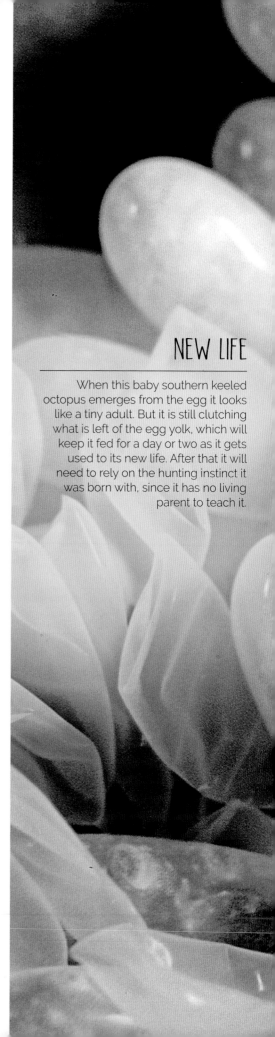

NEW LIFE

When this baby southern keeled octopus emerges from the egg it looks like a tiny adult. But it is still clutching what is left of the egg yolk, which will keep it fed for a day or two as it gets used to its new life. After that it will need to rely on the hunting instinct it was born with, since it has no living parent to teach it.

Guarding the eggs
Off the coast of southern Australia, this female southern keeled octopus is guarding her clutch of eggs. Using a natural form of glue, she has carefully attached each egg to an old razor shell lying on the sandy seabed. She will stay with the eggs until they hatch, keeping them clean and fanning water over them to supply vital oxygen. Once the babies emerge her job is done, and she dies.

The body of a baby octopus is almost transparent, but it develops more color as it gets older.

The empty eggs stay attached by slender stalks, which are glued to a heavy shell or stone.

The big, dark eyes of this unhatched baby are clearly visible through the thin, flexible skin of the egg.

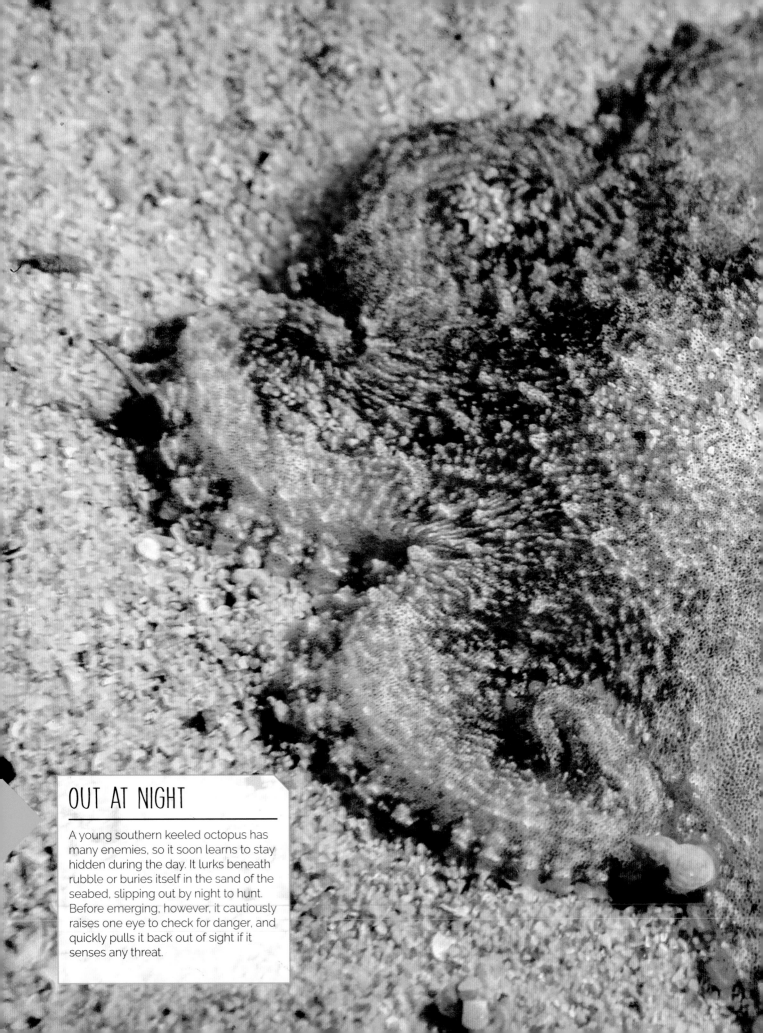

OUT AT NIGHT

A young southern keeled octopus has
many enemies, so it soon learns to stay
hidden during the day. It lurks beneath
rubble or buries itself in the sand of the
seabed, slipping out by night to hunt.
Before emerging, however, it cautiously
raises one eye to check for danger, and
quickly pulls it back out of sight if it
senses any threat.

GLOSSARY

Algae
Plantlike organisms that can make food using energy from the sun.

Amphibian
A vertebrate with soft, moist skin that usually lives in water when young, turning into an air-breathing adult that can live on land. Many return to the water to breed.

Antennae
Sensory feelers on the head of an invertebrate. Antennae always occur in pairs, and they can be sensitive to touch, sound, heat, and also taste. Their size and shape varies according to the way in which they are used.

Bill
A bird's jaws. A bill is made of bone, with a hornlike outer covering.

Bird
A vertebrate that has a hard bill and feathers. Most birds can fly and all lay hard-shelled eggs, for which they often make a nest.

Blowhole
The nostrils of whales and their relatives, positioned on top of the head. Blowholes can be single or paired.

Breaching
Leaping out of the water (usually the sea) and landing back in it with a splash. Breaching is a characteristic form of behavior shown by many large whales.

Brood
A collection of young animals cared for at one time.

Camouflage
Colors or patterns that enable an animal to merge with its background. Camouflage is very widespread in the animal kingdom, particularly among invertebrates, and is used both for protection against predators, and for concealment when approaching prey.

Carnivore
Any animal that eats meat.

Chrysalis
A hard and often shiny case that protects the pupa of a butterfly or moth. Chrysalises are often found attached to plants or buried close to the surface of the soil.

Colony
A large group of animals, such as penguins, that live close together.

Crèche
A group of young animals of about the same age, produced by different parents. One or more adults guards the crèche. This behavior is found in penguins, flamingos, ostriches, and rheas.

Crop
In birds, a muscular pouch below the throat, forming an extension to the food pipe. Its purpose is to store undigested food, and it enables birds to feed quickly so they can digest their meal later in safer surroundings.

Crop milk
A milklike fluid rich in fat, protein, and vitamins, produced by adult flamingos, emperor penguins, and pigeons to feed their nestlings.

Dorsal
Describes something near or related to an animal's back, such as a fin.

Egg tooth
A small hornlike growth that young reptiles and birds use to tear open their eggs from the inside. It usually goes away after the animal's first molt.

Embryo
A young animal or plant in a young stage of development.

Exoskeleton
The tough external skeleton of an animal such as an insect.

Fertilization
The union of an egg cell and sperm, which creates a cell capable of developing into a new animal. In external fertilization, the process occurs outside the body (usually in water), but in internal fertilization, it takes place in the female's reproductive system.

Fish
An animal with a backbone that usually spends its whole life in water and breathes using gills. Many fish have a bony skeleton, but fish such as sharks and rays have flexible skeletons made from a material called cartilage.

Fetus
A developing animal that is partly formed and approaching the time when it will be born.

Fledge
In young birds, to leave the nest or to acquire the first complete set of flight feathers. These birds are known as fledglings, and may remain dependent on their parents for some time after fledging.

Habitat
The place where animals, plants, and other living things are found. Habitats can be on land, or in water. Many species live only in particular types of habitat.

Herbivore
An animal that feeds on plants.

Horn
In mammals, a pointed growth on the head. True horns are hollow sheaths of keratin, covering a bony horn core.

Incubation
To keep eggs warm so they can develop and hatch.

Insect
An arthropod with six legs and three body parts. Most also have wings.

Instar
One of several early stages in the life cycle of arthropods, between molts.

Instinct
A type of behavior that an animal inherits from birth and does automatically, rather than through learning. For instance, newborn mammals use instinct to suckle milk.

Invertebrate
An animal without a backbone.

Keratin
A tough structural protein found in hair, claws, and horns.

Larva
An immature but independent animal that looks completely different from an adult. A larva develops the adult shape by metamorphosis; in many insects, the change takes place in a resting stage that is called a pupa.

Mammal
One of a group of warm-blooded, often hairy vertebrates with females that feed their young with milk.

Marsupial
A mammal that gives birth to young at an early stage of development and usually carries them inside a pouch.

Matriarch
The female in charge of a group of animals.

Metamorphosis
A change in body shape shown by many animals—particularly invertebrates—as they grow.

Migration
A journey to a different region, following a well-defined route. Most animals that migrate do so in step with the seasons so they can take advantage of good breeding conditions in one place and good wintering ones in another.

Molt
Shedding fur, feathers, or skin so that it can be replaced. Mammals and birds molt to keep their fur and feathers in good condition, to adjust their insulation, or so they can be ready to breed. Arthropods, such as insects, molt in order to grow.

Nectar
Sweet, sugary liquid made by flowers. Insects and birds visit the flowers to drink the nectar.

Nutrient
A substance essential for life to exist and grow.

Nymph
An immature insect that looks similar to its parents but that does not have functioning wings or reproductive organs. A nymph develops the adult shape by metamorphosis, changing slightly each time it molts.

Plankton
Floating organisms—many of them microscopic—that drift in open water, particularly near the surface of the sea. Planktonic organisms can often move, but most are too small to make any headway against strong currents. Planktonic animals are collectively known as zooplankton.

Poison
Any harmful substance. Many animals have poisons in their skin to protect themselves from predators.

Predator
An animal that catches and kills others, known as its prey. Some predators catch their prey by lying in wait, but most actively pursue other animals. See also *Prey*.

Prey
Any animal that is eaten by a predator.

Pride
A group of lions that live and hunt together.

Regurgitate
To bring back food that is not completely digested from the stomach to the mouth.

Reptile
An animal with a backbone that has dry, scaly skin, such as lizards, snakes, turtles, and crocodiles. Most reptiles lay eggs with leathery or hard shells.

Sap
A sugary liquid produced by plants. It moves around inside the trunk and branches, a bit like blood in animals.

Savanna
A habitat of wide, open grasslands in a hot, tropical part of the world. It may have scattered trees. The largest savannas are in Africa and South America.

Soaring
In birds, flight without flapping of the wings.

Spawn
Eggs laid by a fish or an amphibian, usually in water, with a jellylike coat.

Species
A particular type of animal, plant, or other living thing. For example, the lion and cheetah are different species of cat. Members of the same species can breed together to produce young, but they usually cannot breed with other species

Spinneret
The nozzle-like organs that spiders use to produce silk.

Termite
A type of small insect that looks much like an ant, feeds on wood, and lives in big groups called colonies. Each termite colony makes a large nest from earth or clay.

Territory
The part of an animal's habitat that it defends from rival animals, usually of its own species.

Troop
A gathering of one kind of primate, such as monkeys.

Tropical
Relating to hot regions.

Tusk
In mammals, a modified tooth that often projects outside the mouth. Tusks have a variety of uses, including defense and digging up food. In some species, only the males have them—in this case, their use is often for sexual display.

Vane
In most feathers, the flat surface on either side of the central shaft. The vane is largest in wing feathers.

Venom
Harmful liquid made by an animal. Venom is different from poison, because it is delivered by stingers or a bite into prey or an attacker's body.

Vertebrate
An animal with a backbone. Vertebrates include fish, amphibians, reptiles, birds, and mammals.

Weaning
In mammals, the period when the mother gradually ceases to provide milk for her young.

Whisker
One of the long, stiffened hairs growing on the face, and particularly around the snout, of many mammals. Whiskers allow animals to sense vibrations in the water or air and are used as organs of touch.

Yolk
The part of an egg that provides nutrients to the developing embryo.

INDEX

ACKNOWLEDGMENTS

The publisher would like to thank the following people for their help with making this book:
Samantha Richiardi for design assistance, Zaina Budaly for editorial assistance, Sarah MacLeod for proofreading, and Helen Peters for indexing.